Unmasking Sexual Con Games

Helping Teens Identify Good and Bad Relationships

Also from the Boys Town Press

Books

Common Sense Parenting
The Well-Managed Classroom
Teaching Social Skills to Youth
Effective Skills for Child-Care Workers
Building Skills in High-Risk Families: Strategies for the Home-Based Practitioner
The Ongoing Journey: Awakening Spiritual Life in At-Risk Youth
Working with Aggressive Youth
Caring for Youth in Shelters
Rebuilding Children's Lives: A Blueprint for Treatment Foster Parents
Boys Town: A Photographic History
Finding Happiness in Faith, Family & Work

Audio/Videotapes

Helping Your Child Succeed
Teaching Responsible Behavior
Videos for Parents Series
One to One: Personal Listening Tapes for Teens
Sign With Me: A Family Sign Language Curriculum
Read With Me: Sharing the Joy of Storytelling with Your Deaf Toddler

For a free Boys Town Press catalog, call *1-800-282-6657*.

Parents or children in trouble or having problems can call the
Boys Town National Hotline anytime, toll-free, at 1-800-448-3000.

You Can Help Teens Identify Good and Bad Relationships

with *Spirituality at Risk: Unmasking Sexual Con Games* Workshop

Unmasking Sexual Con Games equips young people with the skills necessary to recognize and respond to cons perpetrated by "emotional groomers" (people who seek to set up the young person to be victimized sexually).

As a youth care worker, you'll learn techniques designed to enable young people to recognize and avoid abusive and dangerous relationships. The materials and information presented in this workshop were created and proven through their use with at-risk young people at Boys Town.

Unmasking Sexual Con Games is now being used to help teens throughout the United States in schools, churches, and other youth-serving agencies.

Call Boys Town for more information about arranging an *Unmasking Sexual Con Games* workshop for your staff – **1-402-498-1899.**

Unmasking Sexual Con Games

Helping Teens Identify Good and Bad Relationships

**By Ron Herron and
Kathleen M. Sorensen**

BOYS TOWN, NEBRASKA

Unmasking Sexual Con Games

Published by the Boys Town Press
Father Flanagan's Boys' Home
Boys Town, Nebraska 68010

ISBN 1-889322-04-0

Publisher's Cataloging-in-Publication
(Provided by Quality Books, Inc.)

Herron, Ronald W.
      Unmasking sexual con games : helping teens identify good and bad relationships / Ron Herron, Kathleen M. Sorensen. – 2nd ed.
      p. cm.
      ISBN: 1-889322-04-0

      1. Sexual ethics for teenagers. 2. Sex instruction for teenagers. 3. Teenagers–Sexual behavior. I. Sorensen, Kathleen M. II. Title.

HQ35.H47 1997   306/7'0835
                                 QBI97-40339

Table of Contents

Introduction

"If you love me, prove it."

"I'm going to make you feel good."

"You want it, you know you do."

"Just this once."

"What's the big deal? Everybody does it."

Language can be a powerful persuader. When someone is tricked into a sexual encounter by what another person says, it is called a "sexual con game." The term "con game" (confidence game) is defined as a swindle in which a person is defrauded after his or her confidence has been won. Anyone who is coerced into a sexual experience has been defrauded both emotionally and physically.

This manual examines the kinds of words and actions that can be used to seduce, trick, or force teenagers into a sexual relationship. Included in the text are excerpts from more than 50 actual letters written by teenagers to other teenagers. The letters are used as examples to teach young people to recognize the games others play to convince teens to have sex. The more educated and aware our kids are about sexual con games, the more they will be able to avoid and "unmask" the con artist.

Depending on the context, the con artist can also be referred to as the "perpetrator," the "predator," the "player," or the "abuser." Other slang terms include "pimp," "G man,"

"mac daddy," and so on. There may be differences in the intensity of the physical or emotional relationship, but all con artists are guilty of creating coercive relationships. Some con artists knowingly manipulate and convince others to engage in sex. Some simply mimic the actions of the role-models they have seen and are unaware of what healthy relationships are. Although these tactics can be used by anyone of any age, we will concentrate on helping teenagers become aware of how others may threaten or damage their healthy moral and sexual development.

This manual was first published for use in a Boys Town High School religion class consisting of all girls. Many of these girls had been sexually abused and emotionally manipulated by adults or other teenagers before coming to Boys Town. Due to their backgrounds, they were very familiar with the types of behavior described in this manual, and learned to recognize the ways sexual con artists had taken advantage of them.

But sexual con games, harassment, or even abuse, is widespread and can affect youth of any age, attending any school. It is not restricted to age, race, or gender. For example, a national survey conducted by researchers at Wellesley College's Center for Research on Women, published by *Seventeen* magazine and reprinted in *USA Today*, revealed startling rates of sexual harassment in our schools. More than 4,200 female students in grades 2 through 12 responded.

The survey found that of the respondents:

- 39% were harassed at school every day during the last year.

- When administrators or teachers were informed of the harassment, the school took action in only 55% of the cases.

- 89% were subjected to sexual comments or gestures.

- 83% had been touched or grabbed.

Girls also wrote about incidents such as the following:

- "I've been sexually harassed for almost three years.... One guy kept trying to feel me up and go down my pants in class.... It breaks down your soul and brings you down mentally and physically."

  – 14-year-old, New Hampshire

- "There was a guy in my art class who thought it was his privilege to grab my butt whenever he wanted. Like a fool, I thought it was just 'flirting' or 'teasing' but it still made me feel dirty and violated.... No human being should be subject to such degradation."

  – 15-year-old, Texas

- "My harassment came from one boy. Constantly. He was really into smacking my bottom, among other things and always asking me to go to bed with him.... I didn't want to go to school."

  – 14-year-old, Illinois

- "The guys would want you to let them touch you all over.... The school and the principal wouldn't listen to me."

  – 13-year-old, Kansas

The information in this manual can help teens learn how to deal with people who attempt to harass or coerce them into having sex. We cannot turn our backs or close our eyes in the hope that sexual harassment and sexual con games will just "go away." Teenagers will not just "grow out of it." Manipulative boys are not just "being boys." Manipulative girls are not just being "flirts." Somehow, somewhere, teenagers lost the innocence of childhood and the joy that comes with healthy relationships. It is our responsibility to teach our teens what is acceptable behavior and what is not. Above all else, we must teach them that sexually using and abusing another person is morally and legally wrong and will not be tolerated.

The material contained in this manual can be a springboard for some very interesting and frank discussions about teenage sexuality. An open, yet disciplined classroom or discussion group can be a valuable forum for teens to learn about their own sexuality and how to avoid being used.

Some of the information in this manual also is included in the Student Guide. Adult leaders and teachers should decide how the other information that is presented should be used. While the content issues presented in the Leader Guide and the Student Guide are the same, the wording in some sections may be different. Therefore, it is important that leaders read and become familiar with the material in both manuals before they begin a class.

Suggested lesson plans for teachers can be found on page 55. The curriculum is broken down into sessions that focus on specific topics relating to the concepts described in this book. It is strongly recommended that the information in this manual be used in a single-gender classroom. Many students could be uncomfortable discussing sensitive topics in front of the opposite sex. Also, sexual con artists may react to someone "breaking up their game" by revealing their manipulative techniques.

Warning!

Some of the material in this manual is controversial. Although many of the letters are subtle, some contain language that is offensive and vulgar. The letters are not included for shock value, but to show the reality of the language heard and spoken by some of today's teenagers.

In some of the letters, the perpetrator's con game will be obvious to adults. However, these same letters, when written to an unsuspecting and vulnerable teen, can be a potent enticement. (The letters are presented with original grammatical and punctuation mistakes in order to retain their authenticity. Some graphic obscenities have been deleted or edited. Names have been deleted entirely.)

The manner in which you decide to use the letters and information in this manual is left to your judgment. Please be prudent. Some adult leaders prefer to pick and choose certain sections to use in their classrooms. Some adult leaders choose certain letters but delete any offensive language. Others use the manual in its entirety.

It's important to consider the age and developmental level of the students. Other crucial concerns could include a school administration's or youth organization's attitude toward the material, parental and community response, and the amount of cooperation adult leaders have from their students' parents.

One of the primary issues, however, centers around your own attitude and openness toward teaching students about exploitive sexual behavior. You have to be comfortable with the material and be able to present it in an open, caring, honest manner, without resorting to "scare tactics" or condemnation. Your intent should be to inform and guide your students, not moralize or preach. If presented properly, this manual can help young people learn about the cruel games sexual con artists play and how to avoid being used by such people.

The chapter entitled, "Emotional Grooming of Sexually Abused Youth," contains valuable information about discovering and dealing with sexual abuse. This material also contains pertinent and effective information for adult leaders to use with **all** students.

Helping students learn about sexual matters is sometimes a delicate issue. But when the information is presented in an appropriate and sensitive manner, it can empower students with knowledge that will allow them to build healthy relationships and avoid the hurt and shame that results from being sexually used. This must begin with learning how the sexual con artist operates and how to unmask his real intentions so his game loses all its power.

Chapter 1

Emotional Grooming

When a person manipulates someone's emotions and skillfully gains control of the victim, we call that process "emotional grooming." Emotional grooming is used to seduce, coerce, or "con" other youth into sexual activity. Grooming is a preparation, a process where the "groomer" – the person who tries to gain control of another person – tries to trick, convince, or coax a victim into some form of sexual behavior.

Sometimes, these tactics are deliberately and carefully thought out and planned. Other times, groomers merely mimic what they have seen, heard, and learned from others. In almost all cases, groomers don't know how to create a healthy relationship and usually have a warped and egocentric view of what others can do for them. They most likely learned their behaviors and other misinformation about relationships from peers, media, or adult role models. Most have never seen or experienced the mutual respect and selfless behaviors it takes to create a healthy male-female relationship.

Regardless of the level of culpability, if the groomer is successful, the victim usually ends up in a sexually abusive relationship. The groomer gains control of the victim both physically and emotionally. (Although an emotional groomer can be of either gender, masculine pronouns are primarily used in this book for the sake of readability.)

The process of emotional grooming can occur at any age. Young people who have not developed distinct and healthy personal boundaries are very vulnerable to a groomer's tactics. Many teens do not fully understand the psychological, emotional, and social impact of engaging in sexual activity. The emotional groomer attempts to teach them that sexual activity is not only acceptable but also expected. He uses seduction, bribes, or threats to teach this "lesson." Although victims may know something is wrong, the groomer establishes and maintains a position of power and authority. Many adolescents who end up in such manipulative relationships were conditioned at an early age to "please" others no matter what. The groomer takes full advantage of this trait. Other victims are so starved for attention, for someone to care for and protect them, that they will ignore or dismiss the physical or emotional coercion and manipulation just to "have a boyfriend."

Youth who fall prey to emotional grooming are often talked into doing things that are immoral or illegal just to please the groomer. Many times, young kids become victims because they aren't as physically or emotionally strong or aware of manipulation as adults or older kids. Many kids who are sexually abused are conned into believing that this is the way they **should** behave. They are told repeatedly that sexual activity is the way to show love, and they believe it. They are convinced that having casual sex is expected and accepted, and is something they should do to earn love. The emotional groomer also could use his tricks to get other things from his victim – money, drugs, booze, power, possessions, and so on. The key element, however, is that the groomer creates a relationship where he's in charge and can take advantage of his victim through any means that work.

Learning about emotional grooming tactics will help youth figure out when someone is trying to use and abuse them. That's the first step. They have to be aware. They need to recognize the groomer's tricks, or "con games," and use this knowledge to protect themselves or help a friend avoid such people.

This material on emotional grooming is not presented to make kids fearful of being abused by everybody. They need to realize that there are many good and trustworthy people in their lives who want what's best for them. They certainly can learn to develop healthy and wonderful relationships with other people. But the reality of today's world mandates that we make them aware that there are some people who are out to please only themselves. We don't want to let our kids get hurt emotionally and physically by someone they believed they could trust.

Emotional groomers are skilled at manipulation. They are users. A groomer will try whatever is necessary to convince a youth of his undying love and that he is "the man." Often, the victim desperately wants to feel protected and wanted, and this desperation makes the groomer's task even easier. By the time a victim feels or realizes that something is wrong, the groomer quite probably has enough control over the victim to get what he wants.

Emotional groomers actually are perpetrators. The word perpetrate means to be responsible for carrying out a crime. And that's exactly what taking advantage of someone for sexual purposes is – a crime. The emotional groomer is the worst kind of thief. He steals a young person's youthfulness and happiness; he robs young victims of the innocence and safety to which they are entitled. He covers his tracks by leaving his victims confused, humiliated, and ashamed.

The following material is designed to help teens understand how groomers go about emotionally preparing and shaping other people's behavior in order to use them. Teens should understand that the groomer wants control. Teens also need to know that there are ways to avoid these controlling sexual con games. The groomer is skillful in playing his game but that doesn't mean the victim is powerless. The more a teen knows about how to recognize sexual con games, the easier it will be to unmask the groomer and see his game for what it really is.

Characteristics

There are no specific physical characteristics that identify emotional groomers. A groomer could be male or female, a teen or an adult, a college graduate or a high school dropout. It's what the groomer does and says – his behaviors and words – that can alert a teen to his con game.

Most often, people think of emotional groomers as males because they are more sexually aggressive. This isn't true all of the time. There are **many** females who use sexual con games to get what they want. For the sake of easier reading, we refer to the groomers as males in this text. Just remember, **a groomer or a victim could be anyone of either sex**.

Emotional groomers sometimes disguise their con games with normal, caring behaviors in order to mask their real intent. For example, most friends give gifts to one another as an expression of how much they care. It makes the giver feel as good as the receiver. That's normal. The groomer, however, gives his victim a present because he wants something in return. Every time he does something for his victim, he chalks it up as something his victim owes him. He runs a system of sexual debits and credits, and expects to be paid in full.

Groomers may be "slick" talkers. They may be skilled at intimidating others. They may have "status" at a school or with a group of peers. They may have money or access to drugs or alcohol. Regardless of how they play their con games, groomers take emotional and physical advantage of others.

The groomer repeats words and behaviors in order to successfully control his victim, with little regard for the harm that could result. The groomer is tuned in only to his own needs and desires, and is confused about friendship, sex, and love. Many groomers live in families where there is little love and care. They may have been rejected by parents or loved ones, and often they've been abused themselves. They may have suffered the pain of being used and decided that it's time to inflict some pain on others. Many have grown up with little or no knowledge of normal emotional or physical boundaries. But regardless of why groomers do what they do, the end result is that they hurt someone else.

The Emotional Grooming Process

There are two key elements that the emotional groomer must have in place in order to successfully control someone else – a false sense of trust and secrecy.

False Sense of Trust – The first stage of emotional grooming is developing a false sense trust. A groomer convinces his victim that he is the only person in the world who can real-

ly be trusted. The groomer swears that his life revolves around the victim – "You're all I think about," "You're my everything," "You're the only one who really understands me." At the same time, the groomer also tries to convince his victim that he is (or should be) the most important person in her life – "I'll always be there for you," "No one could love you the way I do," "I'll always protect you."

The groomer also attempts to build trust by saying over and over that this relationship is safe and natural – "Everything is all right, don't worry, I'll take care of you." The groomer usually does take care of his victims; he may buy them gifts, or protect them from others, or treat them with favoritism. The groomer skillfully connects much of what he does with the word "love" – "This is the way it's meant to be. This is what real 'love' is all about." The victim is easy prey once she feels sure that the groomer is loyal and trusting, and is convinced of his "true" feelings. Throughout this process, the victim's loyalty is tested and the groomer's control is strengthened. After a groomer successfully weaves this web of false trust, his next step is to get the victim to take part in some form of sexual or immoral behavior. The victim is assured that having sex not only is okay, but also is the "right" thing to do.

In healthy relationships, trust develops slowly and gradually. The emotional groomer, however, tries to rush everything; he's in a hurry to convince his victim that she can depend on and confide in him. The groomer talks alot about trust, but allows no time for a real sense of trust to develop. The groomer also spends a great deal of time telling his victim why others should not be trusted. The victim slowly starts thinking that her life is in his hands. She thinks of him as a protector and friend and savior.

Teens who are starving for attention and affection are prime targets for the emotional groomer. People with healthy boundaries realize that they can trust others in some areas of their life, but not all areas. Teens with poorly established boundaries are not as logical, and the groomer convinces them to not only trust him, but trust him **totally**. Once again, teens who want to be loved are easy prey for all of the lines the groomer uses. In reality, the groomer is creating a false sense of trust. It certainly is not the trust that is present in healthy relationships. It is really an unhealthy dependence that is created by manipulation and deceit.

As mentioned earlier, this book contains excerpts from actual letters written by one teen to another. These letters illustrate how groomers go about developing a relationship with their victims. The following excerpts illustrate how the groomer tries to create a false sense of trust.

"...I just want to talk to you in private with no one else around so I can tell you how I really feel. I won't do anything else, I promise. You will know that I can be trusted when you get to know me better. I would never hurt you or anything like that...."

"...No matter what happens to us I just want you to know if you need anybody to love or just talk to when you are down. I will always be available...."

"...I'll treat you right and I'm not going to do anything behind your back. You are what I live for. So without you my soul is black and my heart is empty. It might sound like I'm trying to get over on you but I'm not. I mean everything I say. It comes from the heart. I cry almost every night hoping I could be with you. You're the best girl I ever had...."

"...We can't let anyone break us apart. If we get into an argument or disagreement we will work it out. People here can't be trusted. Only trust me...."

What makes these lines believable? First of all, a sexual con artist will say these things over and over. He doesn't give up. He figures the more he says something, the more likely someone will fall for his game. He also will use other devious behaviors that are designed to prove how trustworthy he is. It is extremely difficult for some unsuspecting teens to see through these words and actions to find the truth.

Secrecy – The second stage of emotional grooming is developing secrecy. Groomers persuade their victims to keep "our little secret" safe from others – "No one, absolutely no one, can know about what we do." This is one of the few times the groomer gives realistic reasons – "I'll have to move away," or "We'll both get in trouble and not be able to see each other again." The groomer does understand that he would be in trouble either legally or morally. For example, if the girl is a minor, he could go to jail; that's one of the reasons he works so hard to keep the relationship a secret. At the same time, however, he could be bragging to his friends about his "conquest" or how he "scored."

Another way the groomer develops secrecy is by telling the victim that their relationship is different from anything anyone else has ever experienced – "No one could possibly understand how deeply we love each other. We couldn't explain it. Why spoil everything by trying to tell them how we feel?"

Sometimes, groomers use force or threats to make sure the victim won't talk – "If anyone finds out, you'll regret it for the rest of your life," or "You tell anyone and you're dead meat." Other times, the threats involve other meaningful people in the victim's life – "You don't want your little sister to accidentally get hurt now, do you?"

The groomer often does not have to carry through on any threats. Looks, stares, glares, or other body language can keep the victim under his control. Once the victim is afraid because of what might happen if the secret is discovered, she will do almost anything to keep it hidden. The victim is trapped. If anyone finds out, she believes she could be hurt or in trouble. She feels that the groomer holds all the power. If she wanted to end the relationship and promised never to tell anyone, the groomer would never believe her. He would continue to use whatever methods were necessary to keep the relationship a secret. Finally, the victim feels that the situation is hopeless and that she's powerless to do anything about it. She begins believing that it's better to say nothing than to risk making everything worse, and she falls deeper and deeper into secrecy. The following excerpts illustrate how the groomer tries to keep the relationship from being discovered.

"...But then if it does we can still be secret lovers. And no one would have to know about it and it would just be our little secret. You know how much I care about you and hope you feel the same way...."

"...the main thing is that you just tell me about things and don't tell no one about us. I promise you that we will have some good times. Don't let the teachers see you writing letters. Write in private! ...Don't worry about getting scared off by all the rules. But don't say anything to anyone, it's our secret...."

"...I won't do you wrong. Just trust me and no one else. Don't be goin' to no one else cause they'll only do you wrong. This is just between you and me my love...."

"...The feelings we have for each other are true. And will stay that way. If we start going out, we can't let others get in our way. Just remember I really do care about you in many different ways and I've fallen in love with you. You're all I want. We have to be honest with each other. And we can't tell anyone about us. You know how fast stuff spreads around here. Let's just keep it to ourselves and no one will ever need to know...."

Alcohol and Drugs

Before talking about other tricks the sexual con artist uses, it's important to understand how often alcohol and drugs are part of the grooming process. Drug and alcohol use affects both the emotional groomer and his victim. For example, the groomer may use it as an excuse – "I didn't know what I was doing. I was so out of it," or "Don't blame me, I was drunk." Drug and alcohol use also can make the groomer more aggressive and more likely to use force to get what he wants.

Drugs and alcohol make the victim easy prey for the sexual con artist, too. Many kids begin involvement in sexual behavior while under the influence of drugs or alcohol. Most teens will say they use drugs to loosen up, to relax, or to shed the feeling of being nervous around others. All of those things may happen, at least temporarily. Drugs and alcohol impair judgment and make people do what they normally wouldn't do. Things that may seem harmless or fun when a person is high are real problems when the person sobers up.

Many kids become prime targets – easy "marks" – when they are using drugs. Using alcohol and drugs makes a person think that sex is forgivable and allowable – at least during the time the person is using them. In fact, a victim may try to tell herself how mature and "cool" she is, and look on other teens who don't "party" as being "out of it." This attitude makes the sexual con artist's goal that much easier to achieve. Actually, the victim is using the same lines on herself as the con artist used on her. But when the victim is sober, she may be filled with guilt, shame, and regret because of what she did while under the influence of drugs. And it's not uncommon for the con artist – the guy who said all of the nice things when he was trying to get the girl high and have sex with her – to call her a slut or whore the next day.

It is the belief of some teenagers, boys in particular, that it's okay to force sex on a girl when she is drunk or stoned. It isn't. Kids have to understand that it is wrong. Completely wrong. And attitudes like that are dangerous. Forcing someone to have sex should never be a part of a relationship, no matter what the circumstances are. Forcing sex on someone is a crime. It is rape.

Some kids develop real problems with substance abuse. They want to escape pain at all costs. What may have appeared "fun" and a way to relax when they first started, now becomes the only way they know of coping with the problems in their lives. A self-destructive cycle begins. Using drugs makes them loose enough to think that having sex is okay. Using drugs also is a way of forgetting the truth – that it really wasn't okay. All people need to know that life can be tough and there will be times when they experience pain. We can prevent some pain, but we can never escape it totally. What we can do is find healthy and constructive ways to deal with it. Certainly, alcohol and drugs only cause more pain in the long run, both emotionally and physically.

Language Cons

"Language cons" are the words and phrases – or "lines" – groomers use to trick and manipulate their victims. Language cons

sometimes make a victim feel special or desired; other times they make a victim feel guilty or threatened. These lines may seem genuine or sincere when a victim first hears them. Unfortunately, their real purpose is to control the victim. Language cons are used to convince victims to do things they shouldn't do. Although these words may sound obvious or innocuous to adults, they can be very seductive to an unaware teenager. Ultimately, they also make victims feel powerless and helpless because they are repeated so often and are usually connected to some kind of consequence that the groomer controls. When kids hear things over and over, they are more likely to give in to what the groomer wants.

These lines are common language cons:

It's okay. Don't worry.

Just this once. Trust me.

You know I wouldn't do anything to hurt you.

This is normal. This is the way it's supposed to be.

If you love me, prove it.

During the early stages of emotional grooming, the groomer uses language cons to gain the victim's trust and develop secrecy. They may seem harmless at first, but they help the groomer gain control. As trust develops, the groomer feels more comfortable using sexual phrases and vague references to sexual contact. The groomer may start out by using words that only hint about sex – "If I had you alone... Man, you wouldn't believe how good I could make you feel."

As the emotional groomer gradually progresses through the trust and secrecy phases, the language progresses also. The next step may be using slang words when talking about sexual body parts or behavior. Finally, the sexual act itself is graphically described – the perpetrator uses explicit, graphic, and vulgar language to determine whether the victim is receptive to the grooming process. It's like he's seeing how much he can get away with. If the victim doesn't reject him, the groomer thinks he's got a green light to go ahead. If the victim protests, he will back off a little and try some other tactic. Many times, however, the groomer doesn't give up and continues the harassment.

Language cons can seem very innocent or they may be terribly graphic. They may make a person feel good, or guilty, or threatened, or trusted. They may be sly or they may be overt. Most of the time, they are used to trick a person into keeping a secret. They always are used to control another person.

Many groomers want to convince their victims of undying love – "I love you more each day. You're the greatest thing that ever happened to me. My love for you will last forever. I adore you." Some victims are starving for someone to love them, so they are easy marks for the groomer. Most victims want to believe that someone could actually love and protect them, and they become blinded by all the attention they receive. Some victims may not have had a warm and caring home life and want someone to fill the emptiness they feel.

Victims may feel really confused by everything that is happening. At times, they may feel safe and cared for. Other times, they may be a little frightened and worried. Soon, a victim finds that the relationship is frequently on her mind. Even though she may know the relationship has gone too far, she feels powerless or afraid to end it. The giving and receiving of attention becomes something she likes, even though there are other parts of the relationship she doesn't like.

Even though a victim may realize that what the groomer wants is wrong, she may go ahead anyway. The victim has been fooled into thinking that sex and love are the same,

and that you can't have one without the other. If she wants to feel what she thinks is love – the groomer's attention and affection – then she must give sex. That is a distorted view of sexuality. Teenagers must know that the sexual act is not a "duty" nor an "obligation." And premarital sex is no sign of loyalty and devotion to another person. Many victims also don't realize that an emotional groomer may have two or three other victims on the line at the same time. That certainly proves he isn't "loyal" or "devoted."

Aside from convincing a victim to have sex, the groomer often talks her into doing other things that may result in trouble. Running away, drinking alcohol or using drugs, stealing, or getting revenge on someone are things that groomers can convince their victims to do. The grooming process is usually the same – build a false sense of trust and secrecy, then manipulate the person into doing something the groomer wants.

The more socially skilled and adept at emotional grooming the perpetrator is, the less he will rely on physical force. Emotional groomers rarely use physical force to coerce a person into a sexual act. This doesn't mean it hasn't happened. Instead of using physical force to get sex, they rely on the relationship they have established with their victims. Most rape victims experience a trauma that is different from what victims of emotional grooming feel. Victims who have been raped in painful, violent ways see themselves as victims and readily recognize the criminal aspect of rape. These victims know they were not "willing participants" during their abuse. However, many victims of emotional groomers may live with humiliation and embarrassment when they realize how they have been used during the grooming process. Most victims of emotional grooming are not aware of the criminal aspects of the grooming relationship. These victims have been convinced that they are willing participants;

they've even been convinced that they "caused" the relationship. A groomer can twist the truth to make the victim think that the groomer is innocent, that nothing that is wrong with the relationship, or that anything that happens is the victim's fault. The truth is that the emotional groomer is a criminal, a con artist who is just devious and shrewd enough to get away with his crime.

Emotional grooming is a process of manipulation and control. The words a groomer uses are carefully chosen. A groomer says what the victim most needs to hear to get her to do what he wants. The language of a groomer is a con, a trick, a game. The language cons of a groomer are not just "pick-up lines." They are part of a larger plan for using another person. The following characteristics are evident in the language of emotional groomers and perpetrators; this is what sets their language apart from the norm.

- Trying to convince the victim that having a sexual relationship is the same as being in love or the only way to prove love.

- Lust – convincing a victim that it is normal to have an intense sexual desire.

- Coercive properties – using words that threaten or intimidate the victim.

- Possessiveness – treating the victim like an object.

- Repetitiveness – constantly using the same words to gain the victim's trust.

- Referring to sexual behavior as a "duty" or "responsibility."

- Referring to sexual behavior as the ultimate proof of loyalty and devotion.

- Control – using words that reinforce the groomer's position as "the boss."

Even when a victim tries to end the relationship, the groomer will continue to use language cons. He certainly isn't going take

the blame or admit that any type of harmful relationship ever existed. He definitely isn't going to confess that he did anything wrong. He may lie or make threats, or try to convince others that the victim is crazy. Sometimes, the groomer will say that the victim made everything up – "She's always wanted me, but since I didn't pay any attention to her, she just says things to get back at me."

It can be very difficult for a victim to find the best way to stop the abuse. When victims feel powerless and afraid, they are at a loss for what to do. Some victims don't make good choices; they try to solve the problem by running away, hurting themselves, getting further involved with alcohol and drugs, or even attempting suicide. Victims who tell someone who can help, like a trusted adult or older friend, stand the best chance of getting out of the abusive situation. Many victims turn to teachers or counselors for advice.

Many groomers blame their victims for everything that happened – "It was all your fault. You're nothing but a whore! If you hadn't wanted me so much, none of this would have ever happened." This type of verbal abuse just adds to all of the guilt, shame, and hopelessness that the victim may already feel. The victim should realize that the groomer will be just as manipulative trying to get out of the relationship as he was getting into it. Sometimes, other people won't believe what the victim says at first. This is partly because the groomer used language cons with them, too. Through manipulation, he has persuaded other people to believe him. However, if the victim has the courage to tell the truth, and not give up, she is on the road to recovery.

Emotional Grooming Tactics

The following excerpts from letters illustrate the tactics groomers use with their victims. Many of the tactics involve playing on common emotions. The emotional groomer displays powerful emotions to control and get something from his victim. He also **creates** powerful emotions in his victim by what he says and does.

The groomer's ability to find ways to manipulate and coerce his victim allows him to dominate the abusive relationship. Please note that some of these tactics, outside of an emotional grooming relationship, can be normal feelings or reactions. It's the purposeful and coercive way the groomer uses a tactic to manipulate someone that is harmful.

Jealousy and possessiveness. The groomer doesn't want anyone else "messing" with his "territory." This may mean not wanting the victim to talk with other people. The groomer feels he completely owns his victim's feelings and behaviors and is resentful and extremely jealous of anyone who gets attention from his "possession."

> "...I'm telling you now and one time only, I want his stuff out of your locker. What kind of fool do I look like? I'm going out with you, but your ex-boyfriend is still in your locker. No! That is not going to happen. I want his stuff out. Today! If you're my girl his stuff has to go. If you want him it can stay. Your choice...!"

Treating someone like an object to own rather than a person to relate to is at the heart of jealousy and possessiveness. You may see and hear signs of them everywhere – "She's my woman," "You can't talk to him," "You belong to me," and so on.

The emotional groomer also can try to make the victim jealous in order to get her to prove her love.

> "Hey baby, I know you saw me with *****. And I know you don't like me hanging around with her. But if we don't

get it on soon, what's a man going to do? You gotta show me how much you care...."

Teens need to understand that ownership of another's thoughts and feelings has no part in a healthy relationship.

Insecurity. The groomer will use insecurity in two ways. First, he will act insecure and ask for constant reassurance of the victim's love and loyalty to him. The victim is expected to take care of this insecurity by writing love letters or telling the groomer how great he is and how much he is loved. He also may want pity and sympathy – someone to feel sorry for him. This tactic works well with adolescents who are "people pleasers," and the groomer will play on this need in his victim.

> "...I guess it's no big deal. I just don't think I'm really your type or good enough for you. I'm screwing too many things up. I'm not worth it. So let me know if you want to stop our relationship, I'll try to understand. I probably deserve it anyway. The way I treat you, I'm not doing it the way I'm supposed to. I guess I was wrong. I'm sorry for treating you the way I did...."

The second way is to play on the victim's insecurities or create new insecurities.

> "...No one else will ever want you. I'm the only one who is ever going to want you. You'd be stupid to pass up a guy like me... I'm the man. Once I'm through with you, you'll never want anybody else...."

Anger. Most people are familiar with this tactic. Anger is a way to control, or get what you want. Teenagers frequently see and hear it in movies, songs, TV, and unfortunately, in real life. The groomer frequently is angry about something and may argue violently with the victim. This usually leads to him wanting to "kiss and make up," and often, to having sex to "make everything better." Anger can be displayed by yelling, screaming, hitting, or throwing things. The groomer's anger is used to manipulate his victim into a sexual act. Since the victim doesn't want to lose her "boyfriend" or may be afraid that he will take his anger out on her, she agrees.

An emotional groomer who uses anger can be very dangerous. His outbursts may happen more frequently or become more violent. He sometimes connects sex with the power his anger has given him. After awhile, he may believe that sex is good only when someone is hurt or crying. The truth is that whenever anger takes a major place in a relationship, that relationship is doomed.

"...So, he called you? What was his name? I know you at least know that. I've told you not to mess with me! People get hurt when they mess with me. Unless I find out your lying to me. If I find out you are, be ready, because I'm going off. That's why I said if you left something out, tell me now...."

Many times, a victim may blame herself for making the emotional groomer angry. When this happens, she may think she has to have sex with him to make up for it.

*"...Today I seen ***** when I was outside with everyone. He came up there and snatched me up then beat my ass... I fought back, I don't give a f*** who he is... Then after while, my stomach started hurting and I threw up... Later I was laying on *****'s lap and he said he was sorry and we ended up doin' the nasty...."*

Even the language used to describe the sex act is violent. Some groomers describe sex with phrases like "I'm gonna bust your boots," "Let's hit it," "I'm gonna get me a piece of that," "Let's rock it," or "I'm gonna hump your bones." Words like "bust," "hit,"

or "knock" reveal the groomer's true intent – to hurt and use another person. Referring to the other person as an object – "piece of that," "it," or "bones" – enables the groomer to distance himself from the victim and makes it easier for him to use her.

Intimidation. Intimidation is another powerful way to control others. Intimidation means to frighten, coerce, and threaten into submission. The groomer is skilled at intimidating with just a look or a word; glaring or staring can be used to scare or intimidate. He might threaten to hurt the victim or someone she likes. The groomer could take a favorite possession of the victim and hurt or destroy it as a warning of what could happen. These scare tactics usually work; the victim becomes too afraid to say "No." The groomer can be very demanding and harsh, and the victim worries for her safety.

"...I'm not mad at you, as long as you're not lying to me. If I find out you are lying, you and me are finished. So, if you're not telling me something, you better spill it now. I don't want to have to find out later from someone else. I can find out...!"

There also are physical actions that can be intimidating – standing over someone while he or she is seated, standing too close, touching or grabbing someone, using loud and controlling voice tones and language, whispering to someone while pointing at another person, and so on. An emotional groomer might grit his teeth, hit the palm of his hand real hard, snap a pencil in two, or use other aggressive actions to show how mad he is. Guys can take intimidating stances when girls walk by – slouching over, holding their hands on their crotches, making gross signals with their hands, wagging their tongues, or making other gestures that could indicate that they are "nobody to mess with."

14

Accusations. The emotional groomer may accuse the victim of doing all sorts of things that she didn't do. He could say the victim was flirting with someone else or that she was talking behind his back. Accusations also can indicate that the groomer is insecure and needs to be assured that he's the "only one."

> "...just tell me or not if you did anything with *****. If you want him, just go out with him. I'll get over it. It's not like you would really care anyway... ***** even came up to me and said some things about you and him, and what you did. Don't do this to me, even when I hear this stuff, it hurts my feelings. I wouldn't be surprised if you're playing on me. I should of known better. You can't say that I've did anything cause I didn't. You can believe any damned person you want. I didn't do nothin' to her...."

Flattery. Most emotional groomers are "smooth talkers." They know what to say to impress others and appear completely trustworthy. They use language cons that lure the victim into thinking she is the most important person in his world, and that he's the best guy for her. The groomer does not give sincere or honest compliments. He merely uses flattery – exaggerated and insincere comments – to get what he wants. Sometimes, the flattery may be appropriate, but it usually is sexually suggestive or graphic. Even though the groomer's flattery may be insincere and manipulative, the victim may still enjoy the attention.

> "...There's a lot of things I love about you. You're smart, you have a sweet personality and you are very pretty. You are very special to me. Just thinking about you makes me happy. I really want to be there for you. You are too sweet to be taken advantage of and treated bad...."

> "...the world is for both you and I together and no one in between. You don't have to wonder just look into my eyes and my friendship will be right with you.... Your voice is like an angel to me and you're the reason why this boy wants to carry on. I've been living on the sweet things you've said and I don't want to hide it. You are the beautiful picture that I've got in my head and what is stopping us from being alone, I don't know. If I'm the one you love, do you trust me? If I didn't care about you, I would have chosen another girl but I really want you always... Keep 'pretty,' 'sweet,' 'tender,' 'warm,' and compassionate always... I love you girl...!"

We all like to hear nice things said about us. But it's important to know the difference between flattery and praise. Praise simply means showing approval or admiration for people or something they have done. It is specific and truthful. Flattery, on the other hand, is phony and way overdone, and usually is used to get something from someone.

Status. Sometimes, others "look up to" the groomer. He could be a good athlete, have a lot of money, be someone who always has access to booze or drugs, or have a reputation as a tough guy. He uses his popularity and status to lure his victim into a sexual relationship and keep her there. More often than not, the victim will be convinced that she "owes" sex to the emotional groomer because of the attention, popularity, or favors he gives her.

> "...I do like you a lot even though we're not going out. If I didn't would I waste 5 minutes of a phone call on you? Would I call you when there's a lot more girls that I could be calling or would I even talk to you? I'm not too good for you at all because there's no such thing. *****, please believe me I do care and like you and I wouldn't be wasting my time if I didn't...."

Having sex also can be a way to **gain** status. In some gangs, part of the initiation involves sexual conquest; you have to have sexual power over someone in order to join the gang. In that way, you gain the status of being a "real man," a "GQ," or a "stud." Physical force is sometimes used to gain this status.

Bribery. The groomer may give material things to his victim. Giving gifts can be a normal sign of friendship or love, but the groomer gives his gifts purposely to charm the victim into pleasing him. The victim may think that she has to do something to "pay back" the groomer so that he will continue to give her attention and gifts. Sometimes, it may just be the promise of marriage or of always being together that convinces a victim to stay with a groomer. In some relationships, the bribes are alcohol or drugs. This is an old trick used by pimps with their prostitutes: Get them addicted to a substance and they will give you everything you want.

"...If I could do it I'd buy you everything you wanted. Remember that sweater at the mall. That would look so good on you baby. Someday I'll buy it or steal it if I have to. You mean the world to me and I want to show you how much. You just keep being good to me, you'll see...."

"...I know you are coming back from the lake tomorrow. So I will call you and see how you are doing and to talk about our relationship. We do make a good couple if you ask me. I just got me a Michael Jordan jump suit. I was going to try and get you one, but I don't have any money right now. But I get paid 60 dollars Friday if it all works out. ***** will be watching how I spend it so I'll have to think of something. I have fallen in love with you and I mean that. I can't wait to see you because I have something for you and I have to do something. It's a surprise. And I'm not going to tell, I will just wait for the right time. Maybe we can smoke some Js and get truly righteous. I know you like it and baby you're so good then! You get real loose! Anyways, I hope you will like your surprise, I know you will. I've been in the house all day watching TV and being bored. Have you told ***** about us? I know if you tell her or anybody else they would be happy for you. Because a lot of people said we make a good couple and that's the truth. I won't let you get away from me anymore cause I love you and yes I do love you. I can't wait till you see your surprise...!"

Bribery can be very blatant. A 16-year-old girl told this story to her teacher: "How come when I was 13, my boyfriend, who was 19, how come when he took me to the fair, he won me one of those big stuffed teddy bears, and then when we got to his home he told me I had to have sex with him? And how come when he was on top of me, I started crying?" The teacher responded, "You cried because he was taking something precious from you and you weren't ready to give it. That's where the tears came from."

It's obvious that this guy used bribery. He gave her something in order to get something from her. Unfortunately, this attitude appears to be widespread among many boys and men in our society. Many young males – some as young as junior high age – feel that a girl owes them sex if they spend money on the girl. Even more frightening is the attitude that it is acceptable to force sex on a girl if necessary. This type of thinking is devastating to the moral, sexual, and social development of young people.

Control

The goal of all of these emotional grooming tactics is control. The groomer wants to control not only what his victim does, but also how she thinks and feels. He needs to hold power over his victim any way he can. The groomer can use all or some of the tactics we've listed, but his aim is to gain and keep control of his victim. In fact, most emotional groomers will use all of these tactics in combination to get what they want. Some are playing their game with four or five girls. If a particular tactic won't work with one victim, they try it with another. No matter how long it takes, the groomer finds a way to make the victim feel completely helpless and powerless to do anything about it.

"...If you get in trouble doing anything wrong and I hear about it, you will deal with me. I don't want to do anything with any other girl except you. I'm the only one who is right for you. So don't play on me, OK. You wouldn't want to see me mad. Just do what I say. If you're smart you'll listen good...."

"...Listen, this is the topic I wanted to talk to you about. I've noticed since last week you been coming up to me and asking me if I really do love you and I want to break it down to you like this. I really do love you baby and I don't want you to feel like your being pressured into this relationship. But you gotta know that I'm the man. I want you to be positive about this relationship I don't want you to have the impression that if you see me talking to another girl that I'm playing you. I want to be true and I want you to think I'm being true to this relationship. Yo baby I want this relationship to work out if there's anything that you want me to do to show you. Just tell me because I'm willing to do it but you got

to work with me in order to make it happen. I won't do you wrong. Just trust me...."

The following letters are examples of how language cons and grooming tactics were used in one relationship. The first four letters were written by an 18-year-old boy to a 12-year-old girl. He used many of the manipulative methods discussed in this chapter. He said they were going to take it slow. He told her how special she was and how he would always be there for her. He was telling her, sometimes subtly and sometimes overtly, that she should trust him and that he would take care of her. And he told her what she wanted to hear, again and again. Unfortunately, she believed him. The last letter was written by the girl to the boy.

"Hi honey. How are you. When I said I would give you something special, I take that back. I don't want you to think anything about that. I want you to do good cause hopefully you'd feel good and that would make me feel good. Speaking of good asses, you got a nice one yourself. I like you for what you are not what you can give. It's just that sometimes when I'm around you I feel like doing this and that. I want to get closer and stuff and don't do all this negative stuff. Then nature can take its time. Let's get closer but don't go too far. I want you badly. But I will wait if I have to. I have other stuff to say but I don't want to write it down."

"What's up my love? I have been thinking about you night and day. I've been thinking about how much I love you which is a lot. Some other things I've been thinking about is when I first saw you and when I held you in my arms in back of the school. I miss you so much. I can't wait to see you again. There's a lot of things I love about you. You're smart,

you have a sweet personality and you are very pretty. You are very special to me. Just thinking about you makes me happy. I really want to be there for you. You are too sweet to be taken advantage of and treated bad. And I don't want that to happen. I do like to do it, but, we are going to take it nice and slow. You know what I'm saying. Some time I will show you how much I love you, but not right now. Gotta go."

"What's Up? How are you doin' sweetheart? Myself, thinking about you mostly. I wish I could be with you so much. I called you back last night and your mom answered the phone and she told me that I couldn't call you anymore because I was too old to talk to you. I know you don't like that any more than I do but I promise you we will work around that. Because I like you too much and no matter what anybody says, I will always be there for you. Nobody can keep us apart. I want you to be my girl. I want to ask you face to face so you can see for yourself how serious I am. I love you and I want you to be happy. You deserve a lot of tender lovin' care, and I want to be the one to give it to you. That's from the bottom of my heart."

"How are you doin'? Myself, I'm takin' it E.Z. I had a lovely time with you yesterday. You really lightened my day. I want you to know that I think you are a very attractive and sweet person. But, I am a lot older than you and where I come from they call it "robbin' the cradle." You know what I'm saying. Even tho' age is just a number. I still like you and want to get to know you real good. If you know what I mean. I don't want any of these players up here trying to take advantage of you because you're young. I want to be there for you. If anybody gets you, it bet-

ter be me. You're so special to me. Write back. "

(This letter was written by the girl.)

"Hi. How are you? Did you have fun with me last night. Yes or no. I had fun, but I wondered how you liked it? I will always love you baby. My mom found out about us. Now, I can't call boys and they can't call me. But, I will call you, OK? I will find a way. You are the only one who I love. I know I can trust you totally. And, I hope you had fun with me last night. I had never done that before. I hoped you liked it. You are nice and loveable and I think about you every day. I hope you will be there for me. I will give you anything you want and in a big way. If I can't have you I don't know what I'll do. I feel like killing myself right now. And I do hope I kill myself and sorry I said that."

It is evident that the boy had control of this girl. She needed him because he was bigger and older, and she trusted him. She was convinced that he offered her emotional security and protection. This girl had been emotionally and sexually abused as a young child. She thought she had to have sex with someone to be loved. In reality, she was being skillfully manipulated again.

Most examples of language cons presented so far have contained subtle sexual messages. Many have mentioned or centered on love, emotional security, trust, and secrecy. The letter from the following youth is very direct and graphic. Aside from the braggadocio in the letter, it is obvious that this youth is unable to differentiate sexual behavior from affection. Although we may be shocked and disgusted at what the youth says, we have to be aware that some kids talk and think like this. Kids with poor emotional and physical boundaries may even find this language attractive or arousing. It is difficult to teach youth the emotional and responsible side to an affectionate, caring relationship when the sexual act is all they have ever equated to love.

> *"I heard that you are mad when I don't kiss you. The reason why is because I don't want to get you in trouble. So I want to but we can't be out in the open. If you want sex, I give it to you any time, any where. You're not strange about thinking about that, you should keep thinking about that. When I get done with you, I don't know if you would be able to think straight. I also heard you said you had a small gap, I wish I knew that. If it is small I make that m*****f***** bigger, I make your nipples sore too. I would take care of you in all ways. You got a nice ass too. I like it just right. Another reason why sometimes I won't tell you I love you is because if I did you might think one day if I did something wrong to you, you might think I don't love you. That I was just saying that. That is wrong, I need you baby. But if you are serious about getting f*****, just let me know."*

This letter is a reflection of the type of graphic and explicit sexual language used by many of today's teens. Kids consider this language normal because they hear it on television, in music, in movies, and tragically, often in their homes. However, the real fact is that people in our society have become desensitized and are less aware of how dangerous, violent, and degrading such language is.

Chapter 2

Helping Youth Avoid the Sexual Con Game

After sifting through all of the language cons we've seen in the letters from the previous chapters, there is one common theme the perpetrator wants his victim to believe – that he will provide safety and security. A perpetrator will repeat this theme over and over, sometimes subtly, sometimes overtly. Many kids, and especially those who have been sexually abused, have had difficulty building healthy relationships because of the lack of proper love and guidance. These youth usually have low self-esteem and underdeveloped social skills, and are prime candidates for a sexual con artist. Many of these youth also have problems developing relationships with adults, especially parents, teachers, and employers. Therefore, one of the primary tasks for any adult who works with teens is to begin to form positive relationships with them. Here are some helpful hints for accomplishing this goal:

- Use a calm, pleasant voice tone. Kids respond better to an adult who isn't loud, harsh, or punishing.

- Take time to listen and understand. Sometimes, adults tend to view a problem as minor when the problem is a source of true pain for a young person.

- Give lots of sincere praise and compliments. Acknowledge a youth's gifts and talents.

- Be polite and courteous. Thank youth for their cooperation, ideas, or help.

- Use examples to help youth learn acceptable social skills. Explain how to react or what to do in a given situation.

- Give reasons why a youth should or shouldn't behave in a certain way. Kids need to see the link between behavior and outcomes.

- Be direct and honest. Some topics – even those that may be sensitive in nature – are best addressed in an open, factual manner.

- Set (and adhere to) clear rules and expectations. Don't hesitate to correct inappropriate behaviors and set reasonable limits.

- Use your sense of humor. Even in bad situations, laughter can have a healing effect. This can include using appropriate jokes, cartoons, or funny anecdotes to lighten an otherwise serious discussion. Be careful never to appear sarcastic or condescending.

Only by having positive relationships with your students can you begin to teach them the skills they need in order to avoid or escape the sexual con artist. It is our job to educate our youth about healthy relationships as well as harmful relationships. Therefore, we must be living examples of how to create healthy relationships.

Dealing with Language Cons

It is important that youth understand that:

1. Language cons are used to trick, manipulate, and deceive. People who use language cons are selfish and untrustworthy.

2. They can learn how to recognize language cons. Youth need to pay close attention to a person's behaviors as well as his words. The old saying, "A picture is worth a thousand words," applies here. Youth should observe how a person treats others, and listen to what he says to other male friends about dating, relationships, and sex. All of these can be important indicators of an emotional groomer's hidden intentions.

3. They have to learn skills that will enable them to be strong enough to resist giving in to threats or coercion. Young people must build strong relationships with adults they can trust and go to for advice.

4. They should not feel guilt or blame. Sexual con artists need to bear the responsibility for their words and actions. If a teen becomes a victim, he or she should focus on doing things to get better rather than feeling ashamed.

5. There are no excuses for using another person, especially in sexual ways. People who use language cons only want to please themselves, not others.

6. The person who uses language cons most likely will be persistent or try many different angles. The youth has to be just as persistent and not give in.

7. They need good friends of the same gender who can help them hear and see what they may not want to notice about someone else. In other words, friends can help a youth unmask a sexual con artist.

(The section that follows is directed toward the youth and contains suggestions of what they can say to an emotional groomer. These statements are presented only as suggestions of how a youth might respond to a perpetrator's advances. You can lead a discussion on these issues and have youth come up with what they might actually say.)

What Should I Say?

Saying "No" to someone is difficult, especially if that person is skilled at using language cons. Some people are so "smooth" with words that you may not be able to figure out their real intentions. Therefore, it's always wise to stop and think before you agree to do something that may result in negative consequences for you.

Sexual con artists may try all kinds of sweet talk, and this language really works on unsuspecting victims. Sexual con artists can be very persuasive. And, convincing someone to have sex tops their list of priorities.

The following is a list of responses that may help you avoid the verbal traps set by someone who wants to convince you to have sex.

Give me a day to think it over.

You don't really want me; you want sex.

I'm not ready for sex. Don't try to push me into doing it.

If you really care for me, you'll understand.

Love is not sex; love is a commitment to make each other better.

Real love isn't over in just a few minutes.

You don't own my body. And I'm certainly not renting it out.

Love is a two-way street. You only want it one way: your way.

I respect myself. Why can't you?

My brain's between my ears, not my legs.

I want you to love me, not my body.

I want real love, not an imitation.

I have too much to lose.

It's not worth it.

Love is based on friendship, and you don't hurt friends.

I want to be respected, not dejected.

What part of "No" don't you understand?

I know you don't understand, but I want you to respect my feelings.

I care enough about you to do what's best for both of us.

It's not right. I hope you understand.

When I said "No," I meant it.

A Real Example of Saying "No"

This letter was written by a 16-year-old girl to a 14-year-old boy who had frequently written her notes that he gave her at band practice. She was direct and left no doubt about her feelings.

Dear ****,

Hello. I am going to be very blunt and honest with you. NO. I do not like you at all and I have no interest in getting to know you whatsoever.

First of all, you are younger than me and I am looking for different qualities in a guy than what you have. No, there's nothing wrong with you but I want someone different and maturity is a main quality. Please quit writing me notes. No, I'm not going to give you a chance. Yes, you are wasting your time. Sorry, but I'm a blunt person. Lay off.

Yes, I'm your new squad leader, but that means nothing as to how I treat you.

Sorry if I broke your heart.
Very uninterested and sorry,

Using the Questionnaire

The following questionnaire (pp. 25-26) is not a scientific or sociological exam. It is designed only to help teens recognize areas in which they may be vulnerable to emotional grooming. Adapt the completion and scoring of the questionnaire so that it will be most effective for your youth. Your knowledge of their ability to handle such questions will be a key factor in the questionnaire's usefulness. (Additional instructions for using the questionnaire are provided in Chapter 6.)

Some leaders use the questionnaire with individual youth; others use it with the entire group. But it is very important that this information stays confidential. Stress to the youth that answers are not to be shared; this is not a contest. Youth also should not try to look at each other's answers. It may be wise, however, to encourage youth to talk with you or a counselor if they are concerned about the questions or their answers. Also encourage them to share their feelings with their parents.

Each question has an assigned point value. After the youth answer the questions, you can read the point values for each question out loud, give them a master copy of the point values, or use another method to share the point values. These point values are included on the left side of the questionnaire. Then use the scoring key at the end of the questionnaire to help the youth determine how vulnerable they might be. Once again, you should adapt the questionnaire's use to best fit the needs and abilities of your youth.

The next sections – "Ways to Create a Healthy Environment," "Boundaries," and "Relationships" – contain suggestions for positive classroom management as well as information that can be shared with students.

Each section can be used for discussion or written assignments. You also may decide to allow your youth to express themselves in poetry or artwork.

Encourage your students to examine relationships and boundaries. Find examples in everyday life that show healthy or unhealthy relationships. Have them share music lyrics, television themes, plots from movies, or newsworthy current events. Ask students how and why relationships or boundaries have changed over the years. These sections can lead to some very insightful and revealing discussions about the thoughts and actions of your youth.

Emotional Grooming Questionnaire

Have the youth answer the following questions honestly by responding **"Yes,"** **"No,"** or **"Sometimes"** to each question. After the youth have completed the questions, tell them the assigned point value for each response. For example, "On question number 1, Y=5, N=0, S=3." The youth can then total up their scores for all of the questions. A scoring key is provided at the end of the questionnaire.

Y(5) N(0) S(3)   1. Do I want desperately to love someone and for someone to love me back?

Y(5) N(0) S(3)   2. Do I feel like I can't do anything right?

Y(5) N(0) S(3)   3. Do I make the same mistakes time and time again?

Y(0) N(5) S(3)   4. Do I have an accurate knowledge of my body and my sexuality?

Y(0) N(5) S(3)   5. Do I have many friends?

Y(0) N(5) S(3)   6. When I say "No," do others stop what they are doing to me?

Y(5) N(0) S(3)   7. Do I get myself into situations that result in me getting in trouble?

Y(5) N(0) S(3)   8. Do I do things that I know are wrong and later feel badly about?

Y(5) N(0) S(3)   9. Do I worry a lot about pleasing other people?

Y(5) N(0) S(3)   10. Do I worry a lot that I will hurt someone's feelings?

Y(5) N(0) S(3)   11. Do I feel sex is the main way to express love for another person?

Y(0) N(5) S(3)   12. Do I think before I act and avoid situations that I know may cause me problems?

Y(0) N(5) S(3)   13. When I get into a situation that I know is wrong, can I find a way out of it?

Y(5) N(0) S(3)   14. Do I make excuses for things that I've done?

Y(5) N(0) S(3)   15. Do I lie in order to avoid consequences for what I've done?

Y(5) N(0) S(3)   16. Do I ever feel like I have to do something sexual when I'm around members of the opposite sex?

Y(5) N(0) S(3)   17. Do I get other people in trouble by spreading rumors or convincing them to do something wrong so that it takes the "heat" off me?

Y(5) N(0) S(3)   18. Do I believe that having sex will make me feel better?

Y(5) N(0) S(3)   19. Do I ever feel ashamed or guilty after having sexual contact with another person?

Y(5) N(0) S(3)   20. Do I ever feel like one part of me is good and the other part of me is totally bad?

Y(5) N(0) S(3)   21. Do I frequently want to avoid other people and just be alone?

Y(5) N(0) S(3)   22. Do I ever think about having sex with another person because of promises or gifts that he or she gave to me?

Y(5) N(0) S(3)   23. Do I feel like I need to have a boyfriend/girlfriend to be happy?

Y(5) N(0) S(3)   24. Do I think it's okay for a guy to hit a girl?

Y(5) N(0) S(3)   25. Have I ever allowed someone to threaten me or scare me into doing something wrong?

Y(5) N(0) S(3)   26. Do I believe it is a sign of "true love" when someone acts like they own their girlfriend/boyfriend?

Y(0) N(5) S(3)   27. Can I tell when a guy/girl is using a pick-up line on me?

Scoring key:

82 – 135	Watch out! You are vulnerable to emotional grooming. Learn more!
55 – 81	You are somewhat vulnerable, but you need to learn more.
0 – 54	You are pretty aware! Keep learning and teach others how to avoid being used.

Ways to Create a Healthy Environment

Setting clear rules and expectations early helps prevent problems that can arise when young people discuss sexual situations. Firm, but reasonable, guidelines help each young person learn in an environment that is comfortable, open, and appropriate.

Keep the following suggestions in mind when establishing your guidelines. Remember to state any rules in terms that young people clearly understand.

1. Monitor youth group activities. Have a "healthy" paranoia. Make sure youth are where they are supposed to be and doing what they are supposed to be doing. Keeping a watchful eye on their behavior also allows you opportunities to praise them for following rules and to teach alternative behaviors when necessary.

2. Teach youth how to respond to inappropriate sexual advances.

3. Define appropriate and inappropriate classroom behavior. Let the kids know what your tolerances are and what will be reported to their parents or guardians.

4. Teach youth how to report inappropriate behavior.

5. Encourage participation. Discourage any negative behaviors, such as put-downs, name-calling, or inappropriate facial expressions.

6. Be open to talking about sexual feelings and behaviors. Be a counselor and teacher, not a judge and jury.

7. Have specific rules regarding what can and can't be talked about in class.

8. Spend time listening to and communicating with your youth. Sexuality is confusing and, sometimes, frightening to them.

9. Talk about the wide-ranging effects of having sexual contact – physical, moral, spiritual, legal, and social.

10. Be a good role model. Avoid all sexual innuendoes. You may be engaging in behavior that is misunderstood by your students. Such behavior may even be stimulating to them. Sometimes even a pat on the back can be misunderstood.

Skills to Teach Youth

1. Being assertive – Teach kids how to get their ideas and feelings across without making matters worse. If they are in a situation that can be harmful to them, they have to learn how to say "No."

2. Putting their feelings into words – Suggest they write a poem or short story.

3. Talking to a trusted adult – Teach them what to say without saying too much. Many times when kids begin talking, they don't have the discretion to know when to stop. Adults can provide guidance and support without being judgmental. When kids share their feelings, they are on the right path to getting some help. Adolescence is a tough time; your students may not have had the luxury of appropriate teaching or modeling.

4. Knowing what appropriate touching is – Many sexually abused kids do not know how to express affection. They may be too overt or too private. You have to provide a sense of normalcy.

5. Asking for help – Kids often feel powerless and at the mercy of the adults in their lives. Teach them to share feelings appropriately. They may view a situation as hopeless when there actually are many viable solutions that you can provide.

6. Solving problems – Teach kids to look at a variety of options before reaching a deci-

27

sion. Many kids are impulsive. They need to learn how to be logical and methodical when finding solutions to problems.

7. Dealing with peer pressure – Teach kids to think about what others want them to do and why. Teach them to decide whether something is right or wrong, helpful or harmful. Teach them how to get out of negative situations. Maybe the answer isn't always "Yes" or "No;" possibly it is "Maybe later" or "I'll wait and see."

8. Being a friend – Teach kids what true friends are and how they should behave, and that friendship is a "two-way street."

9. Setting goals – Teach kids that they cannot change the past. They should concentrate on learning new skills that will help them in the future. They need to learn how to set achievable goals and how to reach them.

10. Knowing how to say "No" when they feel that someone is trying to convince them to have sex – Give them words to say when they feel uncomfortable because someone is violating their personal boundaries. Help them role-play different situations. Have them act out a common scenario or an actual incident when someone tried to take advantage of them. Discuss how they could realistically deal with the problem.

The following sections are directed at students and are included in the Student Guide.

Boundaries

There's a certain physical and emotional distance you keep between yourself and others. We call this distance your "boundaries." Boundaries are the limits you have set for other people. Imagine a series of invisible circles around your body that determines how close you will let people get to you.

These circles define your boundaries and determine how much you will share with others and how open you will be in your relationships.

Boundaries let things in and keep things out. They protect your thoughts, feelings, body, and behavior. They help tell you what's right or wrong. When someone crosses the boundaries you have set, your mind tells you that the person has gone too far and you start to feel uncomfortable.

The following are two general areas of boundaries:

Physical. These boundaries protect your body. You decide who can touch you, how they can touch you, and so on. Physical boundaries protect sexual areas of the body as well.

Emotional. These boundaries protect your thoughts and emotions. You decide what feelings you will or will not share with others.

People who don't respect your boundaries are people you shouldn't choose for friends. Have you ever had someone you didn't know very well get too close too soon? Were they standing too close, or bending over you, or touching you, or asking you very personal questions? People who come on "too strong" can make you feel uneasy; that's because they have crossed your personal boundaries.

You begin setting your own boundaries at an early age. Your parents help teach you right from wrong, and how to share personal thoughts and feelings with someone.

For example, people often share their private thoughts with their best friends and parents. They allow them inside their closest emotional boundaries. Relationships with other people are not as personal. Casual acquaintances talk about "light" and nonpersonal topics like the weather, sports, movies, etc. Strangers may exchange only necessary information or no information at all. Boundaries change over time and with different people and situations.

As an example of boundaries, think about riding in an elevator alone. You have all that space to yourself and you can move around as you please. Gradually, other people get on the elevator. You're not as comfortable as when you were alone. More people get on the elevator; someone steps on your foot, you feel scrunched in a corner. You smell someone's breath and body odor. You feel uneasy because other people have entered the space where you once felt comfortable. They are just too close. You feel crowded and uneasy. They have crossed one of your physical boundaries.

The people in this example were strangers. Had they been friends, you may not have felt as uncomfortable. But the same feeling of having your boundaries violated can occur in relationships, too. Friends can violate your boundaries when they share personal information about you with others. When friends violate your trust, they also violate your boundaries.

If you find yourself frequently "getting burned" by friends who tell personal things about you to others, maybe you've got the wrong friends. Or, maybe you've set the wrong boundaries and you shouldn't share as much as you have been.

How Do People Violate Boundaries?

- Interrupting a conversation when you are talking to someone else.
- Taking one of your possessions.
- Teasing or making fun of you.

- Asking very personal questions.
- Touching your shoulder or leg or another part of your body.
- Telling other people stories about you.
- Telling other people private information about you.
- Always being around you – making you feel uncomfortable by invading your "private space."
- Saying or doing things in front of you that you find offensive or vulgar.
- Always trying to sit or be next to you.
- Forcing you into doing something sexual.
- Physically or sexually abusing you.

Inappropriate Boundaries

Appropriate boundaries protect a person's body, thoughts, and feelings. But when appropriate boundaries aren't set, it can create a dangerous situation, both physically and emotionally. Inappropriate boundaries can be too closed (never sharing personal thoughts and emotions with others), as well as too open (sharing many private thoughts or physical encounters with casual acquaintances or strangers). Here are some characteristics of other unhealthy boundaries:

Signs that boundaries are too open:

- Saying too much about yourself too soon.
- Telling acquaintances or strangers your personal thoughts and experiences.
- Public displays of affection.
- Wearing revealing clothing.
- Having sexual encounters with acquaintances or strangers.
- Not being able to say "No."

29

- Standing too close to others.

- Making sexual comments about other people's body parts.

- Trusting strangers.

- Believing everything you hear.

Signs that boundaries are too closed:

- Never sharing thoughts or feelings with anyone.

- Not having any friends.

- Not letting adults help.

- Never asking for help, even when needed.

- Refusing to let trustworthy adults appropriately touch you (handshakes, hugs, pats on the back).

Setting Appropriate Boundaries

Here are ways to set and maintain appropriate boundaries for yourself (or to help friends who may have boundary problems):

- Identify youth and adults you can trust and make friends with them.

- Learn to identify and avoid people who look out only for their own interests.

- Spend time with people who do well in school and at home, who are liked and respected by many people. Be around people who bring out the best in you.

- Learn to say "No" when you're being pressured to do something wrong.

- Trust your sense of safety or danger. These are good indicators of right and wrong.

- Learn how to think through and solve problems before reacting.

- Think about times when your personal boundaries were violated. Who was involved?

- What was the situation? Think of ways to handle the problem if it occurs again.

- Speak up when someone or something bothers you. Talk to adults you can trust.

- Set limits about where you will go, what you will do, and how long you will be there.

- Find ways to tell (or show) others what your personal boundaries are.

If you notice that you frequently feel uneasy or anxious around someone, examine your boundaries. Find out why you feel that way. Then, if it is possible, explain your feelings to that person. Maybe he or she can change. On the other hand, if your feelings go beyond just feeling uneasy, and you feel nervous and afraid, talk to a trusted adult and ask for help. Don't place yourself in situations where you worry about your safety.

Relationships

Now that you are able to better understand sexually abusive relationships and recognize the elements involved in the emotional grooming process, the following questions may help you look at all of your relationships more closely. Be honest with yourself as you answer these questions.

- Does this person try to tell me what to do, how to dress, who to be with?

- Do I spend a lot of time worrying about our relationship?

- Do I ever feel like this person tries to make me mad on purpose?

- Do I ever feel I do more nice things for my friend than he or she does for me?

- Does my friend put unrealistic demands on me? What demands?

- Does my friend ignore me when others are nearby? When does this happen?

- Does my friend try to change me to what he or she wants? How?

- Does my friend do things that hurt me? What?

- Do other people tell me that my friend talks behind my back? About what?

- Do I get into trouble when I do what my friend says? How?

- Do I ever feel ashamed, guilty, or afraid after talking or being with this person?

- Have I quit doing things that I used to enjoy since I've become involved with this person? What?

- Does this person ever threaten or intimidate me?

- Has this person ever given me a gift and expected sexual contact in return?

Frequently answering "Yes" to these questions means that your relationship is on shaky ground. Take some time to figure out if you can correct what's going wrong (or if it's worth it). On the other hand, a lot of "No" answers indicates that you and your friend have a good thing going. See what you can do to make it even better.

Ways to Examine Relationships

- Take your time! Really knowing and trusting someone is built up over many experiences. Never rush into a relationship or allow someone to rush you. Take it gradually. If it is good, it will last.

- Friendships should involve give and take from both people. That doesn't mean you should keep a scorecard of what you and your friends do for one another, but it is a good idea to see if there is a healthy balance there. Evaluate the relationship you have now and try to find that balance. No person should be in control or do all of the taking. In other words, make sure you and your friends have the same expectations for relationships.

- Relationships are just one portion of life. Spending too much time thinking about one relationship takes away from all of the other important things you should be concentrating on. Make sure you take care of the responsibilities you have to your family, school, church, and community. Your friends should respect your choice to do so.

- Realize that relationships constantly change; some will change for the better, some for the worse. Learn how to adjust to these changes without giving up the things you believe in. Strive to be flexible and understanding of others while sticking with the things you know are right.

- Look at past relationships that were positive. Name things that made those relationships special. Then look at relationships that you've had that didn't work out. Although relationships are a two-way street, try to figure out what part you played to make each relationship end up the way it did. Make sure you remember things you learned from past relationships to make a current relationship better.

- Identify positive changes friends have helped you make in your life. Then name the things you do to help make positive changes in others. Always make sure you are encouraging one another to change for the better.

- Write down the qualities of a good friend. Look for those qualities in others. Make sure you develop these qualities, too.

- Write down what people do that you don't like in a relationship. Stay away from people like this in the future. (And don't do these things yourself!)

How to Get Better If You've Been Used

1. Get some help. Talk to someone you trust – a professional counselor, teacher, or another adult who will listen. Call the toll-free Boys Town Hotline at 1-800-448-3000. Counselors are on call day and night to help with your problems.

2. Understand that change is possible. You're not weird or crazy. What happened was not your fault; someone took advantage of you. It's time to begin a new life that's free from abuse.

3. Be honest. Admit that something bad happened to you. Don't make excuses for yourself or the person who used you. Don't hide the secret anymore. The pain will never stop if you don't do something about it. Let the pain end so the healing can begin.

4. Get in touch with your feelings. You may be fearful or anxious. Recognize what you're feeling; expect some strong emotions. Don't keep your feelings bottled up inside. Read books on overcoming negative feelings and put them to work for you. If you're depressed, ask for help; if you're angry, learn to channel that energy to a constructive activity. Don't just feel bad; do something about it!

5. Learn to recognize people and situations that can get you in trouble. Do some problem-solving to find ways to avoid or get away from these negative influences. Identify the situation, think of ways you can handle it, think of the good and bad things that can happen if you choose one of those ways, and then pick the best option. If you have trouble doing this on your own, ask a trusted adult for help.

6. Learn how to deal with stress. Things may worry you; people may upset you. Get involved in positive activities. Join a support group. Exercise. Doing kind and helpful things for others will help you avoid getting bogged down in self-pity.

Putting Your Thoughts on Paper

There are several ways we communicate our feelings to others. Many of us rely on face-to-face conversation and telephone calls for daily communication. Writing notes and letters is also a way to reveal our thoughts to people. And just as there is a right and wrong way to talk with others, there is a right and wrong way to write a letter. The letters you have just read in *Unmasking Sexual Con Games* are examples of the wrong way to write letters. Talking with and writing letters to others should not be done to manipulate people.

Getting a letter from a friend can really brighten your day. It's nice to read a letter in private especially when a friend lets you know what's on his mind. Sending and receiving letters is like having a delayed conversation. You can take time to choose your words carefully without the embarrassment of sharing your feelings in front of others.

Even though you may want to share your innermost thoughts and feelings only with the person you're writing to, there is no guarantee that they will be kept secret. Therefore, it is wise to think before you write.

If you want to build appropriate and healthy relationships, here are some things you can talk or write about:

- What happened in school.

- Exciting events such as concerts, sporting events, vacations, trips, dances, parties, etc.

- Your favorite things such as TV shows, movies, music, books, etc.

- Your opinions or thoughts about a current event or topic such as new school rules, curfews for teenagers, world events, or fads and fashions.

- Sports teams or athletes.

- What you did today.

- Giving honest compliments about someone's personality or something he or she did (not for the person's looks or body parts).

- Thanking someone for doing something nice for you or helping you out.

- Your plans for future schooling or work.

Chapter 3

Emotional Grooming of Sexually Abused Youth

Sexual abuse is an extremely complicated problem. It is possible that you may be the first adult to discover that one of the youth you work with has been sexually abused. It also is possible that this youth will trust you enough to disclose what happened. It is more likely, however, that after years of emotional grooming where the youth has been successfully conned into sexual activity, he or she will hold fast to the "secret." The sexual abuse may come to light only because of the keen eyes and ears of the adults such as you who deal with youth on a frequent basis. Many studies indicate that a lack of adequate knowledge and appropriate sexual information, on the part of both youth and adults, compounds the problem of sexual abuse. All youth need information and education about values, and a positive attitude that allows them to identify and avoid sexual abuse.

People who work with youth should be aware of the signs of sexual abuse and have an understanding of its impact. For those youth who already have been abused, healing is possible only with the help of educated, concerned, and caring adults. That's why the following information is included.

The Emotional Grooming Process

Some youth, especially those who have been sexually abused, seem to be consciously willing to engage in promiscuous sexual activity. It may not be their fault; it may be the only way they have learned to relate to others. Many of these kids have been victims of years of emotional grooming. That is, they have been seduced or "conned" into participating. (Although emotional grooming in this context applies to sexually abused youth, the same tactics are used by sexual con artists in a much shorter, and often more intense, time frame.)

In sexually abusive situations, the process of emotional grooming can begin at any age, but usually starts when the child is not yet able to fully understand the impact of sexual behavior or not yet capable of giving informed consent. The abuser could be a person who is the same age as the child, an older adolescent, or in many cases, an adult. The child may experience pleasurable sexual sensations while the abuse is taking place, but he or she is incapable of understanding sexual feelings or sexual behavior the same way as adults do. Children cannot understand the full psychological and social impact of the sexual behavior in which they are engaging. And, most commonly, a child is not developmentally mature enough to resist the inappropriate sexual advances of an abuser.

Many abusers rely on the advantage of being older and stronger than their victims to seduce, lure, or threaten them into engaging in sexual behavior. The authority and power of the abuser, along with the child's lack of maturity and subordinate position, allow the abuser to coerce the child into sexual compliance. Basically, sex is being forced on a child who lacks emotional, physical, and cognitive development.

Emotional grooming of sexually abused youth usually falls into two categories: reward behaviors (the carrot) and punishing behaviors (the stick).

Rewards may include:

1. Gifts

2. Emotional nurturance and closeness from another person

3. Special privileges or getting out of something that other kids have to do

4. Overt bribery – "You let me touch your breasts and I'll buy you a new outfit."

Punishing behaviors may include:

1. Psychological intimidation – "If you don't have sex with me, I'll sneak in your room at night and rape you."

2. Hitting, slapping, pulling hair, teasing

3. Direct physical force

Possible Indicators of Sexual Abuse

Knowing the characteristics of sexually abused youth may help you identify a victim. Many times, youth have been taught to keep their abuse a secret. The following behaviors may suggest that sexual abuse has occurred.

1. Wrestling and tickling – These can be considered normal childhood behaviors, but they also can take on sexual overtones. Wrestling and tickling can be painful or humiliating, or cause discomfort to the weaker person who is on the receiving end. Wrestling, tickling, or roughhousing can be sexually stimulating and can lead to more explicit sexual activities.

2. Obscene language – Youth, especially young children, who refer to adult sexual activities in very explicit ways may be doing so because this language was used toward and against them while they were being sexually abused.

3. Frequent touching – Although touching may seem harmless, it may lead to more intimate behavior. Touching can be a subtle form of foreplay. A youth who frequently touches adults may have learned this behavior from an abuser.

4. Wearing suggestive or provocative clothing – Extremely tight or revealing clothing can be interpreted as a "come-on" to the opposite sex.

5. Pairing – Youth who wander away from the crowd can be a sign or prelude to a sexual advance.

6. Self-mutilation – tattoos, cigarette burns, hickeys, cuts on their arms. This is a sign of a loss of self-respect and the powerlessness kids feel regarding what happens to them.

7. Combination of violence and sexuality in artwork or schoolwork – Youth express themselves in words, art, and play. Pay attention to subtle signs.

8. Overt sexual acting out toward adults – Be cautious with a youth who appears "too friendly." Many sexually abused youth will associate sexual behavior with adult acceptance and caring. You have to explain and maintain your boundaries, too.

9. Extreme fear or repulsion when touched by an adult of either sex – Youth who have been sexually abused may not associate a nurturing touch with pleasure or safety.

Touching often has been foreplay for them, or has eventually led to a sexually abusive situation. Being touched affectionately by an adult may not be viewed as pleasurable by the youth; it may be viewed as threatening or terrifying.

10. Running away – Kids either run away from something or to something. They may be running away from a sexually abusive environment or to a place they think is safe. Many times, running away will result in sexual or drug-oriented behavior.

Treatment

There are specific therapeutic strategies that adults can utilize in treating youth who have been sexually abused. The most important techniques are consistent teaching, counseling, and genuine support. Some youth, however, may need additional help such as that provided by specially trained therapists.

Therapy provides youth with opportunities to express and clarify thoughts and to work through painful feelings. The following types of treatment are available to victims of sexual abuse and their families: individual therapy, group therapy, and inpatient treatment.

Individual therapy usually occurs on an outpatient basis with a clinical social worker, clinical psychologist, or psychiatrist.

Group therapy is especially helpful with teenage victims. Treatment gives them a chance to overcome some of their feelings of isolation ("No one has ever experienced anything as bad as I have.") and to eliminate the secrecy associated with sexual abuse. In a group, they have the chance to receive support for their feelings and rights, and see that others have learned to act upon these feelings in a positive way. Youth also learn interper-

sonal skills that help make them less vulnerable to being victimized again.

Inpatient treatment is sometimes required for youth who are at great risk for self-destructive behavior. Hospitalization can provide the safety and medical supervision required for youth who are temporarily overwhelmed by feelings associated with their abuse and possible severe mental illness. The desired outcome of inpatient treatment is the return of the youth to an environment that is free of abuse.

Most sexually abused youth need a chance to resolve many complex issues that are associated with their victimization. Among the more common issues are:

Believability. The youth who attempted to disclose the abuse and wasn't believed may need repeated assurance that he or she will be believed now. The youth also needs to know that disclosing the abuse was the right thing to do.

Guilt and Responsibility. Frequently, the abuser will blame the youth for the abuse, saying the youth was seductive and "asked for it." The youth also may be blamed by other family members for breaking up the family, or for bringing shame upon the family. The youth needs to be reassured regularly that he or she is not responsible for the abuse. The victim must know that all aspects of the abuse were the abuser's fault.

Body Image and Physical Safety. Sexually abused youth need to discuss how they feel about their bodies. Many think that their bodies caused the abuse and punish themselves accordingly. They also may need to realize that as a consequence of their abuse, they use their bodies to gain inappropriate attention and rewards. They need to be taught how to respect and care for their bodies. Such supportive learning helps combat the "damaged goods" feeling of being a sexual abuse victim.

Secrecy and Sharing. By discussing what behaviors and thoughts can be shared or be kept private, the youth learns that relationships can be chosen, instead of forced upon her or him.

Anger. The youth needs to honestly explore her or his angry feelings about the abuser. During this process of exploration, youth can learn new and appropriate skills to recognize and express anger.

Powerlessness. The youth needs to learn how to regain a sense of control of her or his own life, rather than being controlled by abusers and others. On the other hand, the youth needs to learn appropriate limits, so as to not overdo it and try to control everything.

Shame. Sexually abused youth often are left feeling contaminated, as if there is something fundamentally and essentially wrong with them. The worst thing that can happen to them, therefore, is for someone else to see or know their basic flaw. Sexually abused youth must own and work through such feelings of shame. This is possible with your understanding and care.

Your Attitude and Behavior Toward Sexually Abused Youth

Many adults find it difficult to talk openly with students about sex. When the subject involves sexual abuse, adults find it an even more formidable task. Many adults choose to avoid the issue altogether, apparently hoping that someone else, someone more qualified or comfortable with the subject, will tackle it. When a person charged with helping children takes this approach, the student will not learn the proper lessons about sexuality.

Sexual abuse is abhorrent. There's no question about that. It violates a child emotionally, morally, and physically. We adults may feel disgust and rage toward abusers and sympathy for victims. But no matter what we feel, we cannot lose sight of the task that confronts us. It is crucial that we, as caregivers, learn how to set our emotions aside so that we can begin teaching our youth.

The first place to begin is to learn to treat sex education as a necessary part of our students' overall education. Of course, any discussion of sex, especially the issue of sexual abuse, should be serious and sensitive. But it need not be frightening, condemning, or condescending. A discussion about sex is neither a lecture on morals nor a forum for slang and innuendoes. Sex education gives our children valuable knowledge that will help them learn how to make healthy decisions regarding future sexual behavior and prevent them from making drastic mistakes. The essence of your teaching is that sex is a natural topic for discussion and should be discussed before youth find out about it through their own sexual experimentation. Ironically, many sexually abused youth say they had never been told what sexual abuse was, let alone that it could ever happen to them. Therefore, education is a key to having youth learn what is and is not sexually appropriate.

Be honest and share information. Unfortunately, some adults think that they will unduly upset students by allowing them to know that terrible things such as sexual abuse occur. They think that it would be much better to shelter kids from this reality. Similarly, youth may not want to disclose information regarding abuse because they think the adults will reject their reports as foolish. As youth see adults avoid the topic, they too learn to hide or avoid talking about it. A cycle of avoidance is developed and the secret of sexual abuse continues. It is healthier to give youth as much information as you can about the tragedies of sexual abuse.

Be open about discussions of both sexual abuse and positive relationships. Negative descriptions of people or relationships need to be balanced with positive descriptions of people or relationships. In other words, youth need not be fearful that everyone is an abuser; they need to know that there also are many caring people with whom they can build healthy relationships. If youth learn both the "good" and "bad," they form a much better perspective on sexuality and will be less likely to be alarmed by any discussion of sexual abuse.

Teach your students the difference between "good" secrets and "bad" secrets. This may take a great deal of time because it involves teaching students how to identify emotions and feelings. In other words, teach about the emotional burden that comes with a bad secret and the good feeling that goes with knowing a good secret that later will be shared with others. For example, a "bad" secret is when a student is frightened or conned into never telling anyone that Daddy and her have a "special" sexual relationship. A "good" secret is when a student knows there is a surprise birthday party planned for one of her friends. There is an enormous difference in the impact these two secrets have on a child's life, yet the child may not be able to distinguish between them. When a youth starts displaying behaviors that signal withdrawal into secret relationships, it may indicate some type of abusive relationship.

Speak in even, matter-of-fact voice tones. When an adult is dealing with a child who has been sexually abused, the child may pick up verbal cues that remind him or her of the abuser's behaviors. Overly emotional, intense behavior may trigger the same type of behavior in a sexually abused child. One of the primary skills you should develop is the ability to handle sexual discussions in a way that promotes openness and seriousness, but does not intimate either sexual promiscuity or

strong aversions to the discussions. This also means that you should not talk to students on "their level." Using anatomically correct language provides children with proper sexual terms. This will require a great deal of teaching on your part because much, or all, of the child's sexual knowledge will have come either from a parent – possibly an abusive one – or from a peer group. This also means that kids will "slip up" occasionally. It is best to gently correct them and let them continue. Any strong reaction of disapproval or disgust at their terminology may work against you; the child may use slang terms purposely to avoid the truth or to change the subject. This is not to say that you should continually tolerate slang, cussing, or any other inappropriate verbal statements; you should constantly teach appropriate language. Any shock value in your response may give the child a recourse to use against you in the future. It is important to use correct language consistently; therefore, it is wise to practice what you're going to say.

Believe what your students tell you. Tell them you are going to trust them. Many times before, people may have told a youth they would believe what he or she said, and then didn't. The youth may have felt betrayed or rejected instead – especially if he or she told someone about being sexually abused.

The way you respond can be an appropriate model for your students. It can help kids who have been sexually abused learn to go beyond their abuse and start to live healthful, constructive lives. It won't be easy. There are numerous problems to face along the way. You may become depressed or angry at times. Sometimes, you may not know what to do next. You may feel enmeshed in the student's problems. Share your feelings with your co-workers. It is likely they will have similar feelings and emotions. Talk with specialists in the field of sexual abuse. They may give you some insight and suggestions that will help you out. Above all else, believe that the service you are providing to sexually abused youth is bringing some hope back into their lives.

Chapter 4

Talking with the Teachers

Kathleen Sorensen, a co-author of this book, and Jim Grindey are religion teachers at Boys Town. Kathleen teaches high school girls; Jim teaches high school boys. Both have incorporated the *Unmasking Sexual Con Games* material into their class curricula.

The following is a conversation with them regarding the impact this material has had on their students.

Has the *Unmasking Sexual Con Games* material made a difference in your class?

Kathleen: Without a doubt. I've used this material for more than five years now. My girls are very receptive to the information and can relate much of it to their personal experiences. Of course, many of the girls in my class have been sexually used or abused prior to their placement at Boys Town. They especially connect with the information regarding emotional grooming.

Jim: Many of the guys I work with were perpetrators themselves. Others have been victims of grooming techniques by girls. There's no doubt that all kids are being sent some mixed up messages about sexuality. All you have to do is turn on the TV or radio to hear that stuff. That's why this material is so powerful. It's very healthy for boys to hear about the harm sexual con games can cause. And it also brings out in the open the various tricks they have used to use girls. Some are shocked and angry at the material because they know

they are guilty of the very thing the book talks about.

Do you encounter a lot of resistance from your students?

Kathleen: Maybe in the beginning of the school year, but I wouldn't say that we have a lot of resistance. I think one of the reasons why is because there are only girls in the class and they have had many negative experiences in their lives. The material sort of brings a kind of catharsis or release for them. If there were boys in the class, I'm sure they wouldn't be so open. Another reason is because I say straight out that I'm not trying to change them into what I want them to be. We want to empower them to make good choices in their lives but we can't make them change. We begin with basic information, we begin with skills, and how to identify what's healthy and what's not. We teach them how to respond to someone who is trying to take advantage of them.

Jim: One of the things I found in teaching the boys is that they started, although it was a slow process, to talk about things that they had never talked about before. And there was no way they would share these things in front of girls. Why? Because of their reputation. And because they didn't want that sense of being vulnerable. But it's very interesting, when you get a group of young men together, how many things they want to talk about after you get through all of that macho stuff, which usually takes about three or four weeks. What I try to do with them is deal with the issue of respect, because that's why they want power – to get respect. They've been disrespected so many times themselves that they are not going to tolerate it anymore. And there is a lot of anger, a lot of rage in these young guys. They have been victims, too.

What kinds of victims do you mean?

Jim: Well, some have been sexually abused. Some won't ever admit that, but it's true. Many have been emotionally or physically abused. They have been given a distorted view of what being a man is all about. They are confused and hurt. They do the wrong things because they don't know any other way. And certainly, they are looking for respect in all the wrong ways. So they must get in touch with their own pain and hurt. Once they are honest with themselves and know what they are truly feeling, then they can empathize with the pain of another person. They need to realize their powerlessness so that they can learn some skills and change their lives for the better.

Kathleen: The girls have been victimized also. Many of the girls I work with have been sexually abused and have poor emotional and physical boundaries. They are people pleasers and, unfortunately, have been coerced or convinced that sex was the way to show love. I have friends who teach in public schools and they deal with a whole population of girls who have been victims also. Not necessarily sexually abused girls, but those who have been victimized by the messages they receive in society. Just as the guys get a macho image of being a man, girls are taught that they must give sex to be loved. Somehow, society shrugged off its responsibility to teach kids right from wrong. It's really sad.

Where do you start with these kids?

Jim: The first step is identifying what is unhealthy. The second step is giving them the skills needed to create healthy, balanced relationships. The Student Guide touches on this and we discuss it at length in our classroom. We talk a lot about the media and the messages teenagers are getting bombarded with. Then we try to sort out the good and bad and really evaluate what the messages are saying. Kids begin to realize that many commercials and advertisements are using grooming tactics, too. They're trying to get kids drawn into a belief system that says they really need to buy something or act a certain way to be loved, admired, and accepted.

Kathleen: We talk a lot about friendship and what it's all about. Many of these kids have not had people who cared for them and helped them out. They didn't experience the reciprocity that friendship has – the equal give and take. And certainly, friendship has a lot to do with respect and honesty.

Jim: Right. Many of our kids have not established healthy relationships, so although it seems very basic, we go through all of the characteristics of friendship. More often than not, kids are searching for someone to offer them security and protection. They're usually duped by the tricks a sexual con artist uses. They want so bad to be taken care of, but like the old song says, they're "Looking for love in all the wrong places."

Kathleen: Exactly. And they want it now. I guess that's another reflection on our society. Fast food. Fast cars. Instant cash. They have been conditioned to expect "instant everything." If it takes too long or you have to work too hard, it's not worth it. They look for the same thing in a relationship. You meet someone and boom! It's instant sexual gratification with no thought about what the sexual act means or any possible consequences.

42

How does the media affect the attitudes and behavior of today's teenagers?

Kathleen: That's a hard question to answer. The media definitely have an effect, there's no doubt about that. Whether it is the strongest message is another issue. Kids' role models, family, and friends have a profound effect also. It's easy to point fingers at the media because it's so blatant. We talk about the women's movement and how it has supposedly brought about equality. Yet if you look at what kids are being offered, images of what a woman should be have gone backward. And I think that's why we'll see abuse and violence on the rise. Look at the TV and magazine images of girls and all you see is body parts. The body is an object to be desired. And so girls dress very provocatively to gain the interest of a boy and he's definitely getting turned on by what he sees. So he acts the way he thinks he's supposed to act and tries to make her his conquest.

Jim: That's an excellent point. Kathleen and I both stress this message to our kids: "Hey guys. Listen up. Men and women are wired differently when it comes to issues of sexual arousal. Men are visually stimulated much quicker than women are." I have to stress the issue of responsibility with my guys. Just because a girl is dressed provocatively does not give me an excuse to do what I want with her.

Kathleen: And I have to address the issue of responsibility with my girls. They have to know that the way they look gives guys a message. And they have to be responsible for how they look. As Pastor Buster Soaries says, "Don't send an invitation to the party if you don't want me to come."

Jim: Right. The responsibility is with the boys as well. The first thing is that a boy needs to know that he's going to be physically attracted to females just by looking. That's normal. He's going to be stimulated. But if he contin-

ues to stare at a girl, he may begin objectifying the girl. She's no longer a person; she's become an object. And a lot of the time, that's the way boys describe women – like a car. Their bodies are analogous to the shape and size and purpose of a car. We want to help them see how damaging and wrong it is to treat people like objects.

Kathleen: The messages kids receive are really disjointed. Ads show bodies from the shoulders down or tight jeans from the back. No faces, no personalities, just body parts. The person doesn't have feelings; he or she is just a body. Advertising feeds on insecurity. It will tell you that you don't look good, or more importantly, feel good until you buy the product.

Do your kids want to talk about love? Do they tell you they are in love?

Kathleen: Sure. They think they are in love. But they don't know the difference between being attracted to or infatuated with someone and truly loving someone. It's very hard for them to understand. They haven't been taught that real love is a choice, not a feeling. What they're dealing with is hormones that are powering the relationship. Why shouldn't they? Most of what they hear and see tells them to "go for it." When someone says "I love you, baby," it really means "Let's have sex, baby." I always tell them that the best way to tell if it's love is to wait until marriage to have sex. Whoa! That's a new concept for them. If they can't wait, it's not about love, it's about sex.

Jim: Most of our kids don't know what dating is. I remember distinctly a few years ago in one of my Confirmation classes. We were sitting around talking and one boy says to me, "Mr. Grindey, the purpose of dating is sex." And he was serious. He really believed that. You date to have sex, that's what it's all about. So we have to teach kids over and over that the purpose of dating is friendship, not sex.

What are some behaviors that indicate a girl or boy may be a sexual con artist?

Jim: The most obvious is flattery. Guys get into that game real quick. They hear lines from movies, TV shows, music, and other guys. They seem to have the idea that flattering a girl is the quickest way to prove that they think she is special. And some of these lines are pretty lame. Again, the Student Guide mentions these lines or language cons and gives the "target" some responses to use. One of the things I've noticed is that guys compliment the size or shape of the girl's body.

Kathleen: Most of these compliments are extremely inappropriate. Guys tell girls how big or shapely a girl's body parts are. Like Jim mentioned before, the car analogy is a good one. "Boy, you've got big headlights!" Stuff like that. Girls usually are uncomfortable with that but they aren't used to hearing appropriate compliments. And many girls do like the attention that comes with the flattery.

Jim: Exactly. We have these discussions in class and many of the guys very honestly say that that's what they thought girls wanted to hear. They think that's the ultimate compliment because a girl would think she is sexy and attractive. Girls do similar things by complimenting guys' bodies. Kathleen and I have to start at basic skills and teach them what a compliment is.

Kathleen: Jim and I look for all of the tactics listed in the book. Most of them are pretty obvious to us, but the kids can't see them, or don't want to see them. Another sign is for a teenager to have numerous members of the opposite sex around all the time. There's something going on there; they probably aren't talking about the day's homework assignment. That's what kids call "a player."

Jim: Right. Many of the guys have more than one girl they're trying to play games with. I use the comparison of a guy who has four or five fishing poles in the water at the same time. Sooner or later, a fish is going to bite. If one bait doesn't work, the fisherman will try another.

Kathleen: Girls do similar things. They burn the candle at both ends. They have relationships going with two or three guys at the same time. Many times there are conflicts between the guys or one of the guys and the girl. It can get ugly. But sex, or using sexual con games, is the hook that made them bite in the first place.

Jim: I also look for sexual "posturing." It's quite obvious with guys. You know, the intimidating stances, a guy standing holding his hand on his crotch, standing way too close to a girl, bumping into her, that sort of thing.

Kathleen: Girls do this with boys as well. You might call it flirting, but it's much more suggestive than that. Looking at a guy without ever really making eye contact, but looking at various parts of a guy's body, or whispering to a friend so they both start giggling. Girls and guys sometimes slap or push one another, pinch or hit, or use loud voice tones. Those can be sexual come-ons. Many kids haven't learned what appropriate touching is all about.

Is there hope that we can change the sexual attitudes and behavior of young people?

Kathleen: Sure there is. It all starts with education. We cannot control our kids and tell them what to watch or listen to, who to trust and who not to trust. That's impossible. And I'm not talking about burning books or breaking CDs to make a point. The key is giving our kids enough information to make good choices on their own. They have to be media literate and have the skills to reflect on the messages being sent. They have to have the knowledge to be able to recognize when another person is trying to manipulate them into doing something wrong. They also have to learn how to create healthy boundaries and positive relationships. Some people are going to try to cross those boundaries. Kids have to have enough information, education, and positive relationships with adults so that they can avoid being used.

Jim: We also need to teach them to appropriately handle all of their emotions. We need to help them find constructive alternatives to sex, drugs, gangs, and the like. Both Kathleen and I encourage them to give of themselves, to get involved in athletics, in music, in service to others. We ask them to write personal journals, draw or write, and make posters and buttons; they really get into expressing their feelings in positive and creative ways. All of these things can begin the process of healing and growing.

Kathleen: Yes. There's hope. But we adults need to get started. We need to instill solid, moral principles in our kids. We've got to continue to fight against the negative images that influence our kids' ideas about what it means to be a man or a woman – about how to love and how to be in a relationship. Most importantly, we've got to provide them with the love, respect, and role-modeling they need to become productive, moral citizens.

The Many Faces
of Sexual Con Games

Chapter 5

The Many Faces of Sexual Con Games

Sexual con artists wear "masks" to hide their true intentions. These masks can't be seen like real masks can. They are invisible disguises meant to keep a con artist's games from being known or discovered. These masks come in the form of words, behaviors, or mind games, like making a victim feel afraid or guilty. But if youth learn to look closely, they will see that behind each sexual con artist's mask is someone who wants to use and manipulate them. Victims also wear masks to cover up the shame, fear, or humiliation they feel.

The following passages were written by teenagers who participated in a class that studied the *Unmasking Sexual Con Games* material. The masks and the excerpts you will see in this chapter were created by teens as part of classroom project to illustrate how they felt about being involved in a sexual con game. The students made the masks out of paper mache, clay, or plaster, and painted them to reflect certain feelings and emotions. They then wrote about what the masks meant.

These stories are real. Some kids were victims; some were sexual con artists; some were both. Listen carefully to what they have to say. Listen to the pain they have caused in others or have felt themselves.

What Girls Say

My mask is a groomer who has blue hair – a cold-hearted, red face – angry of being caught, smug look – knowing that he got what he wanted. My mask would say, "Hey baby, would you like to jump in bed with me?" Two hours later: "Ha, ha, I got my way!"

My mask shows the darkness inside and the many changes that we go through when we are being hurt. Burning of the heart – inside. What we can't see behind our smile. My mask would say, "Why me? What did I do to deserve this?"

My mask represents a groomer showing his many colors: overpowering, slyness, evilness. My mask would say, "I'm a great guy. All the girls like me. You'd be missing out if you're not with me." My mask hides the darkness in his life and having low self-esteem and being paranoid about others finding out about him.

My mask is a face that is covered with weird and scary colors. The purple represents the "real" good parts of me. The red symbolizes the wounds, both emotional and physical, that a groomer can cause the victim to feel forever. The orange around the eyes represents how the groomer "blinds" victims and tries to make them see only what the groomer wants us to see. The brown represents the dirtiness and badness you feel as a result of being groomed. The white represents the "unfinished" parts of me that are covered up by the bad stuff. My mask would say, "I feel so lost and abused." I can hardly recognize myself and no one else can recognize me at all. There's too much to remove. I can't find the real me and I'm ashamed of what's happening so I hide behind the mask. My mask hides guilt and fear. It just wants to escape reality.

My mask symbolizes no feelings. The pain and the hurt is shown by the black on the inside. And now I don't feel anything anymore because I've been hurt so much that the black pain is coming through on the outside.

My mask is a guy who says, "I have been keeping my eyes on you. I knew when I first saw you that you were the one for me." Groomers are the persons who do not use their own personalities but they use masks to be someone else.

My mask symbolizes the darkness and hurt feelings that a victim goes through when she is taken advantage of. If it could talk, it would scream "No!" so that the violator will know that no game is going to be played with me. My mask also hides the fear that I will be used again. Hiding the hurt I feel from being used the first time. And the shame, not knowing if it was my fault.

My mask is all black and the face is red. This symbolizes someone in such pain and being so hurt that the pain took over. My mask would say all the feelings that it had inside. It would let others know that this is not the way you should feel. You shouldn't let people to get you into these situations. Look what it has done. It is hiding the truth about a lot of things. There is a lost person that wants to fight back.

My mask would say, "I thought he loved me." He made me experience feelings, but he wasn't feeling the same. My mask is hiding the true person she really is, her shame. The eyes are closed because she doesn't want people to see the window to her soul.

My mask is a mold of myself. The color represents how my life has been divided into worlds. The red shows the pain and the black shows the loneliness and the white shows the acceptance. The tear drops represent how hurt I've been in both areas. My mask hides the pain, hurt, and fright from the world. The uncertain child that could never grow up and be herself.

My mask shows the hurt and pain a person feels inside when she's been hurt and abused. The purple is the bruises she has endured from beatings. The red is the blood she has shed for all the men and the babies she wished to have. The black is the darkness inside. The mixed colors are the cover up to what is really there. My mask hides the shame of letting everything happen to her. The real thing behind the mask is a beautiful strong person who can do a lot of things.

My mask is white with black and red scratches all over it. It has red lips with blood dripping down the right corner. It has red eyes with brown eyebrows. The red is dripping from the right eye and is blood. There is a red bloody gash on the forehead and a purple bruise on the right. There are lights shining off of the eyes and lips. This shows the purity in this victim's face. My mask would say, "I was once pure and can be pure again, but it will take a lot to erase the scars and bruises and get the blood cleaned up." I am mad for what happened but you can believe it won't happen again if I have anything to do with it. My mask is hiding the guilt that is within, believing that it was my fault, the anger felt from the abuse that went on, and the love that could be felt in a real relationship.

My mask is a player who says, "Gosh baby, you so fine... if me and you were alone baby, you'd never want it to stop." My mask is hiding that he doesn't have a lot of respect for girls. He has been sexually abused and physically abused and he's afraid it will happen again.

My mask is a symbol of violation, the dark represents a deep dark heart. I do not like it when I am violated; it makes me feel like a helpless child with nowhere to turn. My mask would say, "Help, get away, I'm telling." It would say that in a voice that has a crying scream. My mask is hiding me; it's a face someone put on me that has dirty feelings and behind it is a person who wants to love. But it is hard to love anyone anymore and to even get close to anyone!

My mask is hiding that they are not interested in your mind; they are looking at your body. Behind this mask, he is just saying, "Man, how fast can I hit on her?"

My mask is split into different colors. The colors are symbols of all the different things that I felt when being violated. The thick black lines that separate colors mean that the feelings are so separate that they stand alone and are very strong. The black eyes stand for blindness and confusion, the disability to see exactly what is being thrown at the victim and to see what this will lead to. The mouth is in the position to kiss, which shows the feeling of needing to be cared for. You'll sacrifice your feelings and self-worth. The eyebrows slanting mean that this victim knows something is wrong. My mask hides confusion, hurt confidence, trapped feelings, indecision.

My mask has red around its eyes – all the redness from crying. The red lines under its eyes symbolize being ready for war (to fight). The white lines and holes symbolize the scars and the beatings. The sad lips could never smile again. The tears never go away.

My mask has bright colors to show how victims may present themselves on the outside. There are dark tears coming from this person's eyes. Their eyes are black – they can't see a way out. Many colors around the face, trying to get out, distorted nose, distorted picture. My mask would say, "Look, can't you see? I'm a person just like anyone else. When you rape me, when you hurt me, it cuts so deeply. I can't get out. I'm trapped. Just go. Please just go. I don't understand.

Please go." My mask is hiding tons of potential, hopes, dreams, fears – all of it's inside. She can't eat or sleep or behave in any regular way. She hides it all behind her mask because she can't let her feelings show at all.

What Guys Say

These masks I wear are just cover-ups for what I really feel. It gets me what I want. I build false relationships. I lie. I lose trust in myself and I can never trust others. I just want things my way and to have no one know how much I hurt inside.

You hurt emotionally and physically. You wear your mask so much you don't know who you really are anymore. You don't know how to get better. And no one wants to be your friend.

I have destroyed relationships. Con games destroy feelings. They destroy personalities. It brings pain. And it also hurts others more.

I hurt myself by getting deeper into the grooming stuff. It is so hard to get out. It just causes you to have grief and can get you locked up if you get caught. You hurt others by using these tactics on them, taking their feelings and respect away. I wish I had never started saying and doing all those things but now I'm trapped and I have a reputation.

The mask I wore said, "Hey baby, I think you look real good. Maybe me and you could get to know each other a little better. Huh, say how 'bout you give me your number and I can give you a call later." These are all the lines I use.

My mask tried to intimidate the girl to go out or do something with me. I would put on the pressure. If I didn't get what I wanted, I'd get very angry. Even though I would hurt people, I knew anger would work and I could get what I want.

My mask had anger and status. My mask tried hard to get what it wanted. If it did not, it got very mad. My mask didn't like it when he used his best bait and you still got away.

First, I would use flattery. Then I would use status. And if that didn't work, I would use insecurity. "What's up marvelous? I'm GQ. Yeah you might have seen me playing football. I did good. Get ready, baby."

My mask would use his gold and silver colors to attract unsuspecting females. He would act cool and calm and use a lot of flattery to lower the natural defense systems of the victim. All through this, he would hide his true self from view as his own natural protection.

First of all, my mask wouldn't let anyone see his "true face." After all, the main purpose of a mask is to conceal its identity. But eventually, it would come out and show its true cares and needs.

My mask would lure his victim in with promises and bribery. Then he would use his victims and their weaknesses to his own advantage. And when they become suspicious of his actions, he let his true self be known and morally crushed the victim until they were so full of pity and guilt that they didn't want to live anymore.

I am hurting the victims beyond repair. They will never be the same persons they were before they met me. By putting them in this situation, I am becoming no better than a rapist, or even a murderer. It takes a long time to work things out for yourself and not be a perpetrator, but it can be overcome, and I can have healthy relationships for the first time in my life.

I hurt myself by not knowing how to talk to girls. It lowers my self-esteem and I don't want to be around other people. I

just take what I want, no matter what. It hurts the other person because she was taken advantage of. So she feels low and worth nothing.

It's not honest. You're lying to other people. You're repeating patterns of pain. They did it to me, I'll do it to them. It's not right but it's what I do.

You hurt yourself because you will become dependent on using the mask. You hurt the other person because you use them. After awhile, the only way you can relate to other people is by using the mask. You will also lower other people's self-esteem. The other person may not trust anyone anymore.

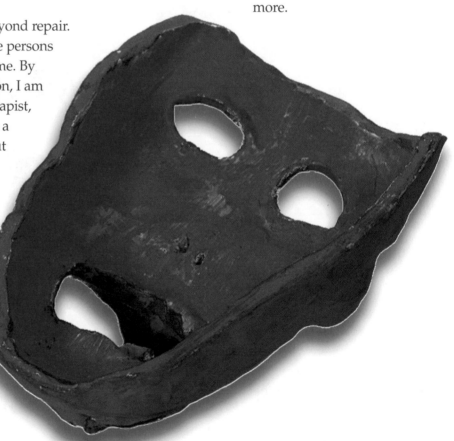

Chapter 6

Lesson Plans

The following lesson plans have been successfully implemented by teachers in a classroom setting. We suggest that you follow these as closely as possible within the context of your work with youth. Adult leaders can use these lesson plans before and during the reading and discussion of the Student Guide for *Unmasking Sexual Con Games*. Adapt the different sessions to fit the emotional, intellectual, and age level of your youth, and the time frame within which you are presenting the material.

We have found that the Student Guide works best when the group reads it aloud together, stopping frequently to discuss or answer questions about the material. We also have discovered that this material works best in same-gender groups; young men and women seem more receptive, ask more questions, and participate more. Below are a few techniques we use when reading and discussing the assignments.

- Each youth has a highlighter and underlines key passages as noted by you.

- Students take turns reading aloud. For variety you can have kids toss a foam ball to the next reader. Or, a reader may call on another student to read next.

- Stop after every paragraph or two and ask for questions or comments. You also could prepare questions based on the day's reading that the youth can discuss or write about in their journals.

- Create notes, reviews, and tests based on what the youth have read and discussed.

Session 1
Introduction to the Curriculum

Goal
To enable youth to understand what this course is about by describing and exploring the concept of a mask.

Leader Preparation
Display a variety of masks around the room, such as Halloween masks, carnival masks, costume masks, or paper mache masks.

Step One – Allow the youth time to walk around and observe the masks. Then ask youth to sit down and discuss the following questions:

- What did you notice about the masks?

- Which was your favorite mask? Why?

- Which mask did you like the least? Why?

- Did you have any particular feelings while looking at certain masks? What did you feel?

- What is the purpose of a mask?

- When might someone wear a mask?

- Why would someone wear a mask?

Step Two – Summarize and make the following points for the group by saying something like:

"For the purpose of this course, we are going to discuss the kinds of masks people wear when they are trying to hide or keep something about themselves from being discovered. We are not talking about real masks that you can see, like a Halloween mask, a carnival mask, or even a circus clown's painted-on mask. We will be talking about 'masks' that are much harder to see. We are going to learn how to identify the kind of masks some people put on in order to use or manipulate others. Their masks are worn to hide their true intentions, which is to use you. Their masks may take the form of words, behaviors, or mind games – like trying to make you feel guilty or scared. But in the end, their manipulative words and behaviors are still a mask, a cover-up, and a con game, all designed to hide from you their true intentions – using and manipulating you."

Step Three – Give each youth a copy of the Student Guide. Introduce the terms "emotional grooming" and "emotional groomer."

Emotional grooming: When a person plays with someone else's emotions and fully gains control of that person, usually in order to coax the person into some form of sexual relationship (p. ? in Student Guide).

Emotional groomer: A person who tries to gain control of another person, usually in order to begin a sexual relationship. Also called a perpetrator or a player (pp. ?? in Student Guide).

Post these definitions on the board or display them on an overhead. You can add to these definitions by stating:

"An emotional groomer wears 'masks' and plays con games. This Student Guide is designed to help you understand what emotional grooming is and how to avoid it so that you can have healthy and happy relationships. This Student Guide will help you to 'unmask' the groomer's con games, or tricks, so that you can see and learn how to avoid the groomer's true intention, which is to use you."

Step Four – Read and discuss the section, "Emotional Grooming," on pages 2-3 in the Student Guide. Remember to stop after every paragraph or two and ask for questions or comments from the group.

Step Five – Have the youth complete these statements, either verbally or in writing. This can include writing in their journals, completing papers to hand in, or a group discussion where everyone is invited, but not forced, to respond.

Something I learned or realized today is....

One question I have is....

Leader Notes

1. Read the entire Leader Guide and Student Guide BEFORE teaching this course. Make sure you re-read the section you are going to cover with your class BEFORE class begins. Jot down helpful notes or questions in the margins of your Leader Guide or your personal Student Guide.

2. Begin each new session with the youth's questions or important points from the last session.

3. If the youth are not asking questions, ask them the questions that you've jotted down in your Student Guide, or ask them for other examples that relate to the assignment.

4. Go to Session 2 once the youth have read and discussed the first five pages of the Student Guide.

Session 2
Emotional Grooming Questionnaire

Goal

To help youth identify indicators of being at risk of falling victim to an emotional groomer. This is accomplished by completing and discussing a questionnaire.

Step One – Begin with any youth questions or important points from previous sessions.

Step Two – Begin by saying: "Today we are going to identify indicators of being at risk of being emotionally manipulated. In a moment, we are going to complete a questionnaire. The questions will help you identify the danger signs of a sexual con game. The purpose of answering these questions is to learn more about yourself and what you can change so that you do not become a victim. You will be the only one to see your answers. Each of you will have an answer sheet. Mark your responses to the questions as I read them aloud. Answer how each question applies to you by writing 'YES,' 'NO,' or 'SOMETIMES.'

"It is important for us to respect one another's privacy. No one should say their answers aloud and no one should look at anyone else's answers. Keep your answers private because this is very personal information. I will not look at your answers, either. Please do not put your name or anything that could identify you on your answer sheet. I will collect your answer sheets after class and throw them away.

"If you do not understand a question, please raise your hand and I will explain it to you. After you have answered all the questions, I will explain how to determine your score."

Step Three – Have the youth take out a piece of paper (or create your own answer sheet) and number it from 1 to 27. Remind them NOT to write their names on their answer sheets. Then start reading the questions from the "Emotional Grooming Questionnaire" found on pages 25-26. Read each question slowly and clearly, pause, and then re-read the same question, as well as the possible responses. For example, say "Question number three, 'Do you make the same mistakes over and over again? Yes, No, or Sometimes.'"

Once the questionnaire has been completed, explain how to score it. Read each question aloud, pause, and then slowly state the numerical value that corresponds to each possible answer. For example, say "For question number three, if you answered 'Yes,' give yourself five points; if you answered 'No,' put three points; if you answered 'Sometimes,' give yourself zero points." Once the youth have totaled their scores, explain the scoring key found at the end of the questionnaire. Remind the youth that the purpose of this questionnaire is to identify the indicators of being at risk to emotional grooming.

Step Four – Go through each question to explain and clarify how each one could be an indicator of being at risk to emotional grooming. Let the youth know that they may ask any questions as long as they are appropriate. You should not allow any questions regarding anyone's personal sexual behavior or experiences. If a youth does ask a personal or inappropriate question, say something like, "This is not an appropriate kind of question for our discussion." Be firm in your response, but do not appear to be sarcastic or belittling to the youth. This is a good opportunity to teach or reinforce what proper boundaries or privacy is all about. If a question could be answered better in a one-on-one situation, invite the youth to set a time to discuss this issue with you.

Remind the youth to use appropriate language when they ask questions or participate in a discussion. Some youth may not know the correct terms for certain body parts or sexual activities. Listen closely to their questions or comments, and ask for more information, if appropriate. Use your best judgment when deciding what is or is not appropriate for the group to discuss.

Discussions should be as general and objective as possible. If a youth does begin disclosing something too personal, ask the youth to stop and tell him or her that you will discuss this matter later in private. If you do choose to talk with a youth privately, make sure that you are not totally alone. Meet someplace where you can talk without being overheard, but where you can still be seen by others. Do not meet behind a closed door. It is possible that lies, rumors, or innuendoes could develop. Adult leaders should not meet alone with youth of the opposite sex. Instead, have another adult of the same sex as the youth continue the conversation, or be present while you meet with that youth.

Step Five – Read and discuss "The Emotional Grooming Process" (pp. 5-10 in the Student Guide).

Remember to stop reading after every paragraph or two and ask the youth for questions or comments.

Step Six – The following questions can be used for written or oral responses. They are designed to gauge learning and to uncover any further questions or concerns.

1. Name the two stages of the emotional grooming process.

2. Explain each of these stages in your own words.

3. Define the word "trust."

4. Who do you trust? Why?

5. How do you decide who to trust?

6. What kinds of things should not be kept secret? Why?

Leader Notes

1. After this session, continue reading and discussing material on grooming tactics in the Student Guide. Ask for questions and comments.

2. Make a poster or an overhead that lists the nine grooming tactics and display them in the classroom.

Session 3
Emotional Grooming and the Media

Goal

To help youth identify the way emotional grooming tactics are presented in TV shows, movies, or music so that youth can identify these tactics in their own lives.

Step One – Begin with a discussion of material that was covered in previous sessions. (Include any pertinent current events that could be used as examples.) You may want to use questions like:

1. What is the most important thing you have learned so far? Why is it important to you?

2. Give an example of an emotional grooming tactic and how it might be used to con someone.

Step Two – Distribute the handout that identifies the nine emotional grooming tactics in media. Explain that the youth will use this handout to identify any grooming tactics they may see in the media.

The following are suggestions for using media presentations with the group.

1. Ask the youth to give examples of what TV programs, videos, or movies they watch or what music they listen to. Then watch these shows and listen to the music yourself, and identify the tactics that they contain. Decide if you want to use a portion of a TV show, video, or movie, or print out the lyrics of a song to use in class. This same process can be used with magazine articles, advertisements, TV commercials, etc.

2. Avoid using presentations that are obscene or beyond the limits of good taste. Sometimes you will have to firmly say "No" to certain shows or songs that the youth want to use in the group. Again, this is another good teaching opportunity, a chance to gently but firmly let the youth know what the limits are. Obviously, you will be using contemporary shows and music that contain material related to sex, dating, and relationships. Set firm limits so you are not presenting material that is too sexually explicit or too violent. (Examples of emotional grooming tactics can be found in most prime-time TV sitcoms and dramas, movies that are geared for a teen audience, and Top 40 songs.)

3. Watch a show or listen to a song several times so that you will be prepared to use it with the group.

4. If you use a song or a music video, type out the lyrics or put them on an overhead for use during the discussion.

5. Use segments of TV shows, movies, or songs. Skip parts that do not pertain to emotional grooming tactics. Cue the video or song to what you want to show or play.

6. Ask the youth to follow these guidelines when watching or listening to a media presentation. Explain these concepts by saying something like:

   • "Respect each other's likes, dislikes, opinions, etc. It is important in this group that we show respect for others by not putting down anyone's favorite kind of music, movies, TV shows, etc. It is okay for you to dislike or disagree with something, and it is even okay for you to express your dislike or opposing opinion on something. But we must do this in an inappropriate manner."

Use this opportunity to teach youth the steps of the skill of "Disagreeing Appropriately." Adapt these steps to fit your group's needs:

Look at the person.
Use a pleasant tone of voice.
Make an empathy/concern statement.
Be specific when telling why.
Give a reason for your statement.
Say "Thank you."

   • "When viewing or listening to a media presentation, everyone should listen carefully without talking. You will have time to ask questions or make comments when the video or song is finished. These two behaviors are important so that everyone can give their undivided attention to what is being viewed or listened to and get the most out of the discussions and activities."

   • Once a discussion begins, only one person should speak at a time. Again, this shows respect for the person who is speaking. It also allows everyone an equal chance to hear one another, to voice their own thoughts without being interrupted, and to pay full attention." (Remind youth what kind of language and comments is permitted, and what kind is not.)

Step Three – Watch (or listen to) media presentations using the handout, "Identifying the Nine Emotional Grooming Tactics in Media" on page 61. Instruct youth to write down any examples of how the nine grooming tactics were used and by which characters. They may write during or after viewing or listening.

Step Four – After viewing or listening to the media presentation, discuss which grooming tactics the youth observed, how the tactics were used, the effects of these tactics, etc. Practice the skill of "Disagreeing Appropriately" and other important discussion skills before beginning the discussion.

Step Five – Ask the youth what the purpose of this session was. (To help the youth identify grooming tactics in popular media.)

Ask questions such as these:

- Do you think a lot of emotional grooming tactics are shown in movies, TV shows, and songs today?

- Can you give some other examples of what you have seen?

- Which methods do you see used most often? How are they used?

- Why is it important to be able to recognize these tactics in popular shows and music?

- How can this information be helpful to you?

One of your goals is to have the youth recognize the frequency of these messages in the media. Another goal is to realize that these manipulative messages are sometimes portrayed as being characteristic of normal dating and marriage relationships.

After the youth have discussed or written their responses to these questions, you also may want them to respond to the following summary statements:

Something I learned or realized today is....

One question or comment I have is....

Something I liked or disliked about today's class was....

Other shows, movies, or songs that have emotional grooming themes are....

Leader Notes

1. After analyzing media presentations for examples of emotional grooming, you may want to create new assignments to show how exposure to these messages affects the thinking and behavior of today's teenagers, especially with regard to relationships with the opposite gender. Have the youth read "How to Deal with Language Cons" in the Student Guide.

2. When the youth have a clear understanding of the nine emotional grooming tactics, continue reading and discussion. Let the youth create role-play situations where they can practice what to say or do if a person tries to use emotional grooming tactics to get them to do something sexual or wrong. Use the suggestions on pages 26-29 of the Student Guide for ideas.

Session 4
Using the Letters

Goal
To enable youth to identify how and why emotional grooming tactics are used in notes and letters that teens write.

Step One – Begin, as usual, with the youth's questions and comments from previous sessions. Ask about any examples of grooming they recently observed in the media.

Step Two – Explain the session by saying: "Today, we are going to continue identifying emotional grooming tactics by looking at some notes and letters that were written by teens to other teens. By carefully analyzing these notes, we can see how the sender tried to con the recipient into some sort of unhealthy or abusive relationship. These are

Identifying the Nine Emotional Grooming Tactics in Media

INSECURITY	FLATTERY
ANGER	STATUS
INTIMIDATION	BRIBERY
ACCUSATIONS	CONTROL

JEALOUSY AND POSSESSIVENESS

After viewing/listening to this media piece, name three grooming tactics you observed. Describe who used them and how.

real letters written by real young people, both male and female, ranging in age from 11 to 20 years old. Their names have been removed to protect their identities. We are going to use some of these letters as examples of the type of language cons that are used in an attempt to manipulate someone."

Please note that you should choose the letters you want to use before your group meets. It is most helpful to photocopy each letter onto an overhead transparency and then display it on an overhead screen for the group. Do not give copies of the letters to the youth; teens might use these letters in an inappropriate manner. Also, note that some of the letters contain sexually graphic or offensive language. Again, use only the letters that you decide are appropriate for the limits of your group.

Step Three – Show the letters one at a time so that the group can read and discuss them. You may ask for volunteers to read the letters aloud, or you may want to read them yourself. It is a good idea to remind the youth that:

1. Only one person speaks at a time.

2. They should show respect for each other's questions and comments (no put-downs).

3. They should disagree appropriately.

4. No one will be forced to express thoughts, feelings or opinions aloud.

Go through several letters. Have the youth point out the grooming tactics they identify in each letter and how they are used. Ask them to identify how the author was trying to build a false sense of trust by sweet-talking, making unrealistic promises, making threats, using intimidation, etc. Use the questions at the bottom of each letter for further discussion.

Leader Notes

You may want to end the session here, depending on how much time you have. If you do end here, make sure you summarize the session by asking the youth to write down or say their responses to the following statements:

Something I learned or realized today is....

A question I have is....

If I could tell other teens one thing about emotional grooming, I would say....

Step Four – Summarize what has been covered so far by saying, "We now know what the emotional grooming tactics are, how they are used, and even how to avoid being a victim. We know what NOT to say or do to begin a friendship or help a friendship grow. So what are we supposed to say and do, especially in friendships with the opposite gender?" Ask the youth to open their Student Guides to pages 37 and 39.

Once kids have read through this section, ask for volunteers to role-play using these communication/relationship-building skills in various scenarios like:

- Meeting someone you'd like to get know better.

- A first date with someone.

- Introducing yourself to a new kid (in your neighborhood, church, school, etc.).

After role-playing, present the following assignments. You can let the youth choose their assignment and complete it individually, or have them work in pairs.

You also could make this a list of homework assignment options:

1. Write three different appropriate notes or letters you could send to someone of the opposite gender. One could be to someone you just met, one could be to someone you

have known for a few weeks, and the last one could be to someone you know well. (Use the Student Guide for ideas.)

2. Ask a mature and trustworthy adult of your gender what he or she thinks are appropriate conversation starters or tips for teens who are just meeting each other. Write down the person's comments and bring them to the next session. (This would need to be a homework assignment.)

3. Write summaries of two more realistic role-plays that would make use of appropriate communication/relationship-building skills presented in the Student Guide.

4. Draw a cartoon or find at least five examples in magazines that show teens using appropriate communication/relationship-building skills in a realistic way.

Step Five – Use these questions for oral or written reflection:

• What did you learn or realize from today's session?

• What should a teen write in a note to someone he or she likes?

(Read pages 41 and 42 in the Student Guide for more ideas.)

Session 5
Setting Boundaries for Healthy Relationships

Goal
To enable kids to identify and set healthy boundaries for relationships.

Leader Preparation
Lay three or four hula hoops on the floor near the group.

Step One – Once everyone has arrived and settled in, begin class with a discussion of the previous sessions. Ask the youth to pre-sent or summarize the projects they completed last session.

Step Two – Ask for a volunteer to stand inside each hoop. (If you do not have access to hula hoops, you can use masking tape to create circles on the floor of your room.) Once the volunteers are inside the hoops, ask the group to take some time to observe the hoops and the effect they have on those inside them. Then ask:

1. "What do you notice about these hoops?" (You will get a variety of responses. That's okay. You just want them to begin thinking about the concept of boundaries.)

2. "Do you notice anything different about the people inside the hoops?" (Again allow for a variety of responses.)

3. Ask the volunteers inside the hoops to pick up their hoops and hold them about waist high around themselves. (If you are using masking tape circles, ask the youth to close their eyes and imagine each volunteer wrapped in a circle.)

4. Continue by asking, "Now that these hoops are surrounding our volunteers, what would you have to do if you wanted to give one of them a hug?" (Allow time for their answers.) Then make this point: "The point here is that when the hoop is surrounding the volunteers, it would be hard to maneuver around it to hug them unless the person inside the hoop cooperates or allows you closer." Thank the volunteers and ask them to return to their seats.

Continue the discussion: "These hoops represent what we are going to talk about today. We are going to call these circles our boundaries. Everyone has their own boundaries. Even though we can't really see them, our boundaries are there to protect us and keep us safe from emotional or physical harm. We learn what our boundaries should be from our parents and other significant adults in our lives. We often learn what a boundary should be without even knowing that we are learning it. Sometimes, though, our parents actually do tell us what our boundaries should be. Can you tell me about a time when your Mom or Dad told you what to do or not to do with strangers?" (Allow the youth to respond.)

Then ask, "Why do you think your parents told you that?"(Allow time for their answers.)

Continue by saying: "Your parents told you what to do or not do with strangers because they were trying to protect you. They were teaching you about the kinds of boundaries you should have with strangers. Can you think of any other things your Mom, Dad, or another important adult has told you about what to do or not do with other people?" (Again, give the youth time to respond. As they name different things they were told, identify and affirm the statements that truly are examples of appropriate boundaries.)

Continue by saying: "There are two general kinds of boundaries. (It would be helpful to have these written on the board or on an overhead.) One kind is called physical boundaries. These are boundaries that protect your physical body from harm. The other kind is called emotional boundaries. These protect your private thoughts and feelings, your inner self. Turn to the section on 'Boundaries' in your Student Guides."

Ask for volunteers to read this section aloud. Remember to stop after each paragraph to ask for their thoughts or questions.

Step Three – After reading, summarize by saying: "We learn about acceptable and unacceptable boundaries not only from our families, but also from society and culture. Appropriate boundaries are good. They help us feel safe, and let us know when we might be in physical or emotional danger. Imagine that the hula hoop represents your physical

boundaries. Your boundaries are like protective hoops or circles around you, letting people as close as is appropriate and keeping out those who should not cross inside your boundaries. One problem in our world today is that some people have inappropriate boundaries, either because they never had anyone teach them proper boundaries, or because their parents or role-models showed them inappropriate boundaries. Either way, there is hope. A person can learn and put into practice new boundaries at any time in his or her life. But that's a decision only that person can make. We can't make changes happen in someone else."

Step Four – After reading about boundaries, continue the discussion by saying: "Imagine a set of circles that represent the different levels of boundaries everyone should have. Notice that YOU are in the center of all the boundaries. This represents your most private and special emotional and physical parts, which should be shared only with certain trustworthy and caring people. Notice that each of the outer circles are farther and farther away from the most private parts of you. This is important. Only certain people should get close to you, both physically and emotionally. Your emotional and physical boundaries protect you and help you keep a manipulative person from getting too close.

"If the wrong sort of person does get too close, your boundaries can warn you of possible harm or danger. How do your boundaries warn you? Usually, you will feel uncomfortable, scared, nervous, very uncertain, or anxious about a person or an experience that is not good for you. You should trust these inner feelings. They are trying to warn you and protect you from possibly getting hurt or used. When you notice those feelings, talk to a trusted adult. Tell the adult what is going on, and ask for help and insights. Then you will begin to see the danger more clearly, and be able to decide what you should do about it.

"Sometimes, you may not pay enough attention to your feelings; in those situations, a friend or family member may sound the first warning. Again, you should listen to the people who care about you and who have earned your trust and respect. They may see something that you don't see. They may notice a potentially dangerous situation before you do. Again, open up to their comments, talk about what is really happening, and look at things from their perspective. Remember, they are only trying to protect you and show care and concern for your well-being."

Step Five – Have the youth answer these questions individually in their journal or notebook.

- Name five important physical boundaries.

- Name five important emotional boundaries.

- Name three positive action steps you can take if someone crosses or threatens any of your boundaries.

- What are three important boundaries for a first date? Why?

- How would you let your date know that these are your boundaries?

- List three examples of inappropriate boundaries. (pp. 33-34)

- Name four ways people violate boundaries. (p. 33)

- Name four things you can do to begin to set appropriate boundaries. (p. 34-35)

Step Six – Invite the youth to share their responses with the rest of the group. Remind the group members to show respect by listening and not putting anyone down. When volunteers have finished sharing, ask the youth these questions:

- What's the most important thing you learned today?

- Why is this important to you?

- Any questions or comments?

Leader Notes

1. By this point in the course, you have almost completed the Student Guide. At your next meeting with the youth, read pages 36-40 and focus on the positive elements of the sections "Ways to Examine Relationships" (pp. 37-39) and "How to Get Better If You've Been Used" (pp. 39-40). You may want to follow up on any related topics that came up and were important to your class. You also could have the youth write and act out role-plays or skits that show how to identify and avoid emotional grooming, how to say "No," and how to set good boundaries.

Followup Activity: Addressing "Dressing"

Goal
To enable teens to recognize how certain clothing styles communicate sexually suggestive messages.

Step One – Divide the class into same-gender groups.

Step Two – Distribute magazines, newspapers, fashion catalogs, or any other materials that depict current clothing styles that are popular among teens.

Step Three – Have the kids cut out pictures of clothing styles they like or think are "cool," even if they aren't allowed to wear those styles.

Step Four – After 15 minutes, ask the kids to choose three to five pictures of clothing styles they like best (for their own gender), and have them glue each picture onto a piece of paper. Tell the youth not to write their names on these.

Step Five – Collect the girls' pictures and give them to the guys' group. Collect the guys' pictures and give them to the girls' group. Make sure each youth gets three to five pictures.

Step Six – Ask the youth to take a few minutes to look at each picture. Have them flip the picture over and write short phrases that come to mind when they look at the picture. Again, the youth should not write their names or do anything to identify who wrote a certain statement. Ask them to be honest and descriptive without being gross or offensive. Have them repeat this process by passing their set of pictures to the person on their right. (Encourage the youth to write something different from what has already been written.)

Step Seven – After 15 minutes, collect all the pictures and ask the kids to return to their original seats. Give the girls the pictures of the female styles and give the guys the pictures of the male styles.

Step Eight – After the pictures and comments have been reviewed, discuss the following questions:

- What do you think was the purpose of this activity?
- What did you learn from this activity?

After discussing the questions, summarize by saying:

"The purpose of this activity was to help you recognize what the opposite gender thinks or feels when they see a certain clothing style.

"As much as we may dislike it, such judging happens all the time. Many people make judgements or assumptions about others based only on what they see – clothes, hair style, body shape, skin color, age, or gender. It may not be fair or right, but it happens. And because we are judged this way, we must be aware of the kinds of judgments and assumptions that are made in these areas. Obviously, we can't control our skin color or body size, but we can control the messages we send through the clothing styles we wear or the body language we use. Some clothing styles are sexually suggestive. (Give some examples.) No matter what, some folks will assume you are willing to "put out" if you're willing to "show it." We need to be aware of and accountable for how we dress, walk, and talk.

"Finally, just because someone dresses suggestively – or even flirts or teases – it does NOT give anyone the right to force sex on that person. We all can control our sexual feelings, just as we all can control the messages we send by how we dress, walk, and talk."

Variation – Invite various adults to anonymously comment on clothing styles, too! Have them select pictures and write their observations on the back in the same manner as the kids.

Chapter 7

Emotional Grooming Letters

This chapter contains letters that illustrate the type of language used by emotional groomers. There are two sets of letters – one with answers to questions that follow each letter (Leader's Answer Key) and one without answers (Letters for Transparencies). Each letter is numbered and corresponds with the identical letter in the other set. If, for example, you choose letter #3 in the letters without answers, you also choose letter #3 in the Leader's Answer Key. You may use the letters in the order that best suits the goals you have for your students.

Leaders have found it useful to make overhead transparencies of the letters to show their students. This prevents letters from being misused or circulated outside of the classroom. **Please do not make copies and distribute them to the youth**. You also may choose to black out any language you feel is inappropriate. You can make copies of the Student Answer Sheet and ask the students to use it when making verbal responses.

The Student Answer Sheet lists possible responses to the following questions:

A. What was this person trying to do?

B. What tactic(s) was the groomer using?

C. How did this person want to make me feel?

D. What did this person want me to do?

E. How would I respond?

(Note: Each of these responses is discussed in the text of the Student Guide.)

Students should determine what language cons and emotional grooming tactics are used in each letter to help them recognize the ways people might try to manipulate them. There may be several appropriate answers. The goal of these exercises is to have the students use a cognitive process to sort through all of the language cons and decide how they would handle the situation.

After your students answer the questions, you can lead a group discussion about their responses. Encourage them to explain what they would do and how they would feel if they received such a letter or if someone talked to them in the same manner. Also, have them explain how their response would change based on their relationship with the other person. For example, the person could be a) a complete stranger, b) a casual acquaintance such as another youth in school, c) a friend or someone they have had several dates with, or d) a close friend or frequent date. An exercise such as this helps the students understand personal boundaries.

Students should be encouraged to share experiences about people who have tried to trick them with language cons. Have them explain how they handled the situation and what the outcome was. Awareness of emotional grooming is a key to helping youth avoid being tricked and manipulated.

Student Answer Sheet

A. What was this person trying to do?

1. Develop my trust
2. Create a secret relationship

B. What tactic(s) was the groomer using?

1. Jealousy and possessiveness
2. Insecurity
3. Anger
4. Intimidation
5. Accusations
6. Flattery
7. Status
8. Bribery
9. Control

C. How did this person want to make me feel?

1. Special
2. Afraid
3. Safe
4. Guilty
5. Sexually aroused
6. Loved
7. (Other feelings I would have)

D. What did this person want me to do?

1. Run away or break a rule
2. Have sex
3. Spread rumors or gossip
4. Apologize
5. Obey
6. Believe everything he or she says
7. Share my feelings
8. Be the "only one" in this person's life
9. (Other things this person wanted me to do)

E. How would I respond?

Leader's Answer Key

Letter 1

Hello cute thing, I thought I'd write because you've written so much in the past and I've not written to you in a while. By the way, don't think that I wrote back to ****** okay. The world is for both you and I together and no one in between. You don't have to wonder just look into my eyes and my friendship will be right with you. I'm not cheating on you and I want you to understand that even though we don't get together much, I really do "love" you. I want just the two of us to hold on the precious moments and you are truly the water of my heart and river. Whenever you tell me that you're crying, I feel that I'm doing something to hurt you and I fell so guilty "but why"? Your voice is like an angel to me and you're the reason why this boy wants to carry on. I've been living on the sweet things you've said and I don't want to hide it. You are the beautiful picture that I've got in my head and what is stopping us from being alone, I don't know. If I'm the one you love, do you trust me? If I didn't care about you, I would have chosen another girl but I really want you always. Let's not let this dream pass us by and let's talk to each other at school more often. You are for me and I'm for you so let's take part in what we want to give to each other. I really don't want you to care so much about me and write so much until your fingers are sore okay "honey"! Take your time gently and remember that I love you because I'm doing this for you and all for love. You're in my mind. Keep "pretty", "sweet", "tender", "warm" and compassionate always. It's not always easy to be a friend but I'm your true friend and "I know what you need"! Please excuse my writing. I love you girl! From none other than yours truly.

A. What was this person trying to do?

1 - Develop my trust

B. What tactic(s) was the groomer using?

2 - Insecurity
6 - Flattery

C. How did this person want to make me feel?

1 - Special
6 - Loved

D. What did this person want me to do?

7 - Share my feelings

E. How would I respond?

Letter 2

I want you to know just because we got in trouble doesn't mean we can't still go out together. We just have to be more careful, that's all. If we keep everything a secret then no one will find out about what we do. Right?

I don't want us to part because it's stupid and it won't solve anything. You mean a lot to me in so many different ways. I love you. Don't let people put things in your head, if you know who I mean. I won't let you go. Don't worry about getting caught, OK? We need to stay together.

A. What was this person trying to do?

2 - Create a secret relationship

B. What tactic(s) was the groomer using?

9 - Control

C. How did this person want to make me feel?

3 - Safe

D. What did this person want me to do?

6 - Believe everything he or she says

E. How would I respond?

Letter 3

How are those people treating my sweetheart. I hope with some respect! I'm glad that you finally got around to writing me. I want you to know that I like you a lot too and like yourself I think of you a lot and wish that I could be with you 24/7. But it gets greater later when you finally get adjusted to this place (I hope soon) we will be spending a lot of time together. There's a lot of rules but I know the way around them. The main thing is that you just tell me about things and don't tell no one about us. I promise you that we will have some good times. Don't let the Teachers see you writing letters. Write in private! I forgive you for lying about your age. Just as long as you learned from it. Always keep me in your heart because you will always be in mine. And I want to keep you happy because that is the kind of respect I give to a girlfriend of mine. And you will be my girl sooner or later but, we both are going to take it nice and slow. If that is OK with you. I have been thinking about you a lot and one of the things is that if you get mad or have an argument again and you run again. I don't want that to happen because you are really special to me and I don't want to lose you. Please try to call me. I have been trying to call you but nobody ever answer the phone.

P.S. You are pretty sexy yourself and you do know how to kiss real good. I want to see a picture of you baby whenever we see each other again. Don't worry about getting scared off by all the rules. But don't say anything to anyone, it's our secret baby.

A. What was this person trying to do?

2 - Create a secret relationship

B. What tactic(s) was the groomer using?

6 - Flattery
9 - Control

C. How did this person want to make me feel?

1 - Special
3 - Safe

D. What did this person want me to do?

6 - Believe everything he or she says

E. How would I respond?

Letter 4

I'm in bed thinking about you. We are not going to break up because of what happened. Because I love you and you love me. Please don't run away because it will make things worse and I don't want to see you get hurt or lose you. Don't change your story. Just remember, we only talked, then did heavy kissing and I started to fall asleep. Don't change your story for nothing, because if your story is different from mine I can get sent away. I don't want to lose you for anything and I want us to be together for a long time. Even after we graduate, so please don't do anything wrong like yell at them or run away. I don't know what I would do if you left me. If I have to leave I will come see you and take you with me where ever I go. You have changed my life a lot in so many special ways. If I can take it here, you can too. So don't think you can't.

A. What was this person trying to do?

2 - Create a secret relationship

B. What tactic(s) was the groomer using?

2 - Insecurity
9 - Control

C. How did this person want to make me feel?

3 - Safe

D. What did this person want me to do?

5 - Obey

E. How would I respond?

Letter 5

What's up chick? I really don't know about what we were talking about after school yesterday. I wouldn't mind, but you know what will happen if we do. How are we supposed to live? I sure couldn't get a job!! What made you decide to leave anyway? Baby, I would love nothing more than to be with you. The problem is if it would be the best thing for us. Is it really what we want to do? You do mean a lot to me, and I hope you know that. If we do go, how will we get our clothes? How do we get from here to there? What happens if me and her boyfriend have a fight and we have to leave? If I leave the cops will be looking for me. I can't stay in the city too long. Unless you want me to got to jail. You would have to get used to me carrying a gun. I don't go anywhere unless I'm packin'. Who is paying for the apartment? How do we get around? Where do we get clothes from? I want to leave here so bad, but I'm not going anywhere unless I know what's up. When are you planning to leave anyway? We would have to figure that out real quick. What if she doesn't get to leave? Then what are we gonna do? Did you think about that? If I leave I don't plan on being caught anytime soon, so I have to know all of this stuff. If we left we could be together as much as we want to though. Couldn't we? We could make love all of the time. As soon as you get me a good answer to these questions, I will tell you if we should go or not. You'll probably go even if I don't. If you did, I would find you and beat your ass!! I love you.

A. What was this person trying to do?

> *2 - Create a secret relationship*

B. What tactic(s) was the groomer using?

> *4 - Intimidation*

C. How did this person want to make me feel?

> *2 - Afraid*

D. What did this person want me to do?

> *1 - Run away or break a rule*

E. How would I respond?

Letter 6

Hey sweetness. Miss me? Well I missed you! Today was my last day in that hell hole. I am so sorry that I made you angry for being there. I'll never ever go back. So were you being good when you didn't have me to cuddle or to make you feel good. Well I felt like I was losing you slowly but surely but I hope and pray that I don't. You'll never never lose me ever. There's nothing here that can steal my heart away from you, my lovely, my sweet. I did miss you a lot. I feel jealous when you sat at the table at lunch with that one guy. I felt that I had really messed up. I hope not cause I will always be with you and make you feel my presence wherever you go. You know how I feel. Hey baby. Listen, I'm gonna get straight to the point when are we gonna hook up at the movies or somethin' so we can do somethin' nasty. Cuz I've been wantin' to do somethin' to you for a long time! Ever since you first came here. So now you know. Write me back to let me know what you have to say. From me. I did call last night!

A. What was this person trying to do?

> *2 - Create a secret relationship*

B. What tactic(s) was the groomer using?

> *2 - Insecurity*
> *6 - Flattery*

C. How did this person want to make me feel?

> *1 - Special*

D. What did this person want me to do?

> *6 - Believe everything he or she says*

E. How would I respond?

Letter 7

I find out Thursday if I stay or have to leave. I hope I stay because of my family back home and you. I told ***** to tell you I love you because I never have the right time to tell you, but I will today. Don't let ***** play with your head. Please don't leave me, I need you more than anything. We both love each other and don't want to lose each other, so we can't let nothing get in our way. You're my sweet thang forever. I want to find you right away and kiss you. Can I get a kiss after school. If I don't I think I will die. I'm glad we fell in love with each other, just thinking back to the first day I saw you. I wanted it to be us. And that's when I fell in love with you. Love at first sight. I knew we would get closer and closer. You mean a lot to me, don't give up on me for nothing. Remember I'm in love with you and I love you and we will stay TOGETHER FOR-EVER.

A. What was this person trying to do?

2 - Create a secret relationship

B. What tactic(s) was the groomer using?

2 - Insecurity
9 - Control

C. How did this person want to make me feel?

6 - Loved

D. What did this person want me to do?

6 - Believe everything he or she says

E. How would I respond?

Letter 8

Hi sellout! Well anyways, about today. Meet me after school for a trip through the career center, to finish something we started. I'm sure you want a reason. Well, my reason is because I'm supposed to be gettin' the boot today for something I did over home visits! If you don't believe me, ask ***** or *****. I really wish we could be together, but *****! All I'm askin' is "can we finish" so I can remember my last day with you? We need to do it now. It's our last chance and besides no one would ever know. Because believe it or not, I began caring for you a lot!

Love = Me

P.S. Please let's do this the real proper way. So let's finish!

A. What was this person trying to do?

2 - Create a secret relationship

B. What tactic(s) was the groomer using?

9 - Control

C. How did this person want to make me feel?

5 - Sexually aroused

D. What did this person want me to do?

2 - Have sex

E. How would I respond?

Letter 9

How are you doin'? Myself, I'm takin' it E.Z. I had a lovely time with you yesterday. You really lightened my day. I want you to know that I think you are a very attractive and sweet person. But, I am a lot older than you and where I come from they call it "robbin' the cradle." You know what I'm saying. Even tho' age is just a number. I still like you and want to get to know you real good. If you know what I mean. I don't want any of these players up here trying to take advantage of you because you're young. I want to be there for you. If anybody gets you, it better be me. You're so special to me. Write back please.

A. What was this person trying to do?

   1 - Develop my trust

B. What tactic(s) was the groomer using?

   6 - Flattery
   9 - Control

C. How did this person want to make me feel?

   1 - Special

D. What did this person want me to do?

   6 - Believe everything he or she says

E. How would I respond?

Letter 10

Hi. How are you? Did you have fun with me last night. Yes or no. I had fun, but I wondered how you liked it? I will always love you baby. My mom found out about us. Now, I can't call boys and they can't call me. But, I will call you, OK? I will find a way. You are the only one who I love. I know I can trust you totally. And, I hope you had fun with me last night. You are nice and lovable and I think about you every day. I hope you will be there for me. I will give you anything you want and in a big way. If I can't have you I don't know what I'll do. I feel like killing myself right now. And I do hope I kill myself and sorry I said that.

A. What was this person trying to do?

   2 - Create a secret relationship

B. What tactic(s) was the groomer using?

   2 - Insecurity
   8 - Bribery

C. How did this person want to make me feel?

   1 - Special
   6 - Loved

D. What did this person want me to do?

8 - Be the "only one" in this person's life

E. How would I respond?

Letter 11

Our relationship is going to last a long time. The feelings we have for each other are true. And will stay that way. If we start going out, we can't let others get in our way. Just remember I really do care about you in many different ways and I've fallen in love with you. You're all I want. We have to be honest with each other. And we can't tell anyone about us. You know how fast stuff spreads around here. Let's just keep it to ourselves and no one will ever need to know. I really care about you and I mean that. Have to get going.

A. What was this person trying to do?

   2 - Create a secret relationship

B. What tactic(s) was the groomer using?

   9 - Control

C. How did this person want to make me feel?

   1 - Special

D. What did this person want me to do?

   8 - Be the "only one" in this person's life

E. How would I respond?

Letter 12

Below is a letter written by a girl from a small farm town to a boy from a big city, more experienced and streetwise than herself. Being less experienced and unfamiliar with the behaviors of a "street kid," the girl was uneasy and a little scared of the boy. Can you identify the grooming techniques the boy in the letter used to manipulate the girl?

This probably makes no sense to you, but I have some things I really need to tell you. I really wish I would have gotten your address. Can you send it to me?

Gosh, I don't know where to begin. I do like you (a lot). I did not know how to react or act around you. Don't get me wrong, it was not because you were black, but because you were a guy. See, I have never had a guy like me. Sure, as friends - most of my best friends are guys! It's just no one has ever done to me what you did. I was very overwhelmed and I did not know what to do. I thought you were so sweet and nice. I did not give you a fair chance. I wish I would have.

I know I am terrible at talking to guys, and I shouldn't really talk. It takes me awhile to get used to people and I took too long. I am so sorry. My mind wanted something with you, but something told me to hold on. Plus, a lot of people in my co-op told me that you would just use me and throw me away. I did not believe them, but I don't know. I really wish I could start over again.

Also, you always wore those sunglasses. I wanted to see your eyes. They were so understanding. I kind of was a little scared when you had the glasses on and your dark clothes and you told me to come there in the student center. You seemed like such a tough guy. I loved seeing your eyes. That's one of the things I loved about you.

I really could not figure you out because you were nice to me and everyone else just thinks of me as a friend. Maybe I am making a lot out of nothing. But I just want you to know I liked you a lot.

A. What was this person trying to do?

2 - Create a secret relationship

B. What tactic(s) was the groomer using?

4 - Intimidation
7 - Status

C. How did this person want to make me feel?

7 - Curious

D. What did this person want me to do?

9 - Want him

E. How would I respond?

Letter 13

So, he called you? What was his name? I know you at least know that. I've told her not to mess with me!!!! People get hurt when they fuck with me. If I was getting another girl's number, that is between you, her and me. How in the hell did ***** get in it!!

I'm not mad at you, as long as you're not lying to me. If I find out you are lying, you and me are finished. So, if you're not telling me something, you better spill it now. I don't want to have to find out later from someone else. I can find out!!

You have to keep your friends out of our business. ***** is getting on my nerves. She is always in our business. Then whoever that was in your house that told you that shit the other day. I don't like shit like that. I don't let my friends get in my business like that. If this is our relationship they have to be out of it.

You are my lady, you will be until you give me a reason to feel differently. I'm not mad at you. You haven't gave me a reason to be. Unless I find out you're lying to me. If I find out you are, be ready, because I'm going off. That's why I said if you left something out, tell me now.

I still love you. I'm not mad at you. I'm gonna go off on *****, though. She is gonna stay out of my business. If not she'll get her ass hurt. I can't stand people fucking around with me. I gotta go. Love ya.

A. What was this person trying to do?

   2 - Create a secret relationship

B. What tactic(s) was the groomer using?

   1 - Jealousy and possessiveness
   3 - Anger
   5 - Accusations

C. How did this person want to make me feel?

   2 - Afraid

D. What did this person want me to do?

   5 - Obey

E. How would I respond?

Letter 14

I'm telling you now and one time only, I want his shit out of your locker. What kind of fool do I look like? I'm going out with you, but your ex-boyfriend is still in your locker. No!! That is not going to happen. I want his shit out. Today! What did you say to ***** today? She is messing with me. She's getting on my nerves. Your friend better go somewhere. If she messes with me I'll fuck her up. You better get his shit out of your locker!! If you're my girl his shit has to go. If you want him it can stay. Your choice. Peace.

A. What was this person trying to do?

   2 - Create a secret relationship

B. What tactic(s) was the groomer using?

   1 - Jealousy and possessiveness
   3 - Anger
   4 - Intimidation

C. How did this person want to make me feel?

   2 - Afraid

D. What did this person want me to do?

   5 - Obey

E. How would I respond?

Letter 15

Hey BABY what's down. Shit, it's 11:45 and I can't sleep at all. Maybe it's because I feel so bad about what I did to you. But maybe we can start all over. We shouldn't have gotten caught. We won't be able to see each other as much. But then if it does we can still be secret lovers. And no one would have to know about it and it would just be our little secret. You know how much I care about you and hope you feel the same way. I love you more than words can say. But it's hard for me to give you my feelings here. Today was the most depressing day I had in my life. When I wanted to listen to the radio all I would hear is songs that made it worse for me to start feeling normal again. But hey, I probably will have a lot more of these kinds of situations.

What I'm going to say is going to be real hard for me to say. But I made many other girls hurt, and cry because I would go out on them or do stupid things. But I really didn't give a shit. All I would do is just laugh when I heard they cried over me. But with you I couldn't laugh or just didn't forget about it. This shows that I really hurt someone who I love and care about. And you've been on my mind all day. And I am very sorry for leading you on like the way I did. And just doing what I did.

But you know I'll take the offer of being together for ever. No matter what happens to us I just want you to know if you need anybody to love or just talk to when you are down. I will always be available. But it is going to be up to you if you want to marry me. Please write back, but be careful that no one knows about us.

A. What was this person trying to do?

   2 - Create a secret relationship

B. What tactic(s) was the groomer using?

1 - Jealousy and possessiveness
3 - Anger
4 - Intimidation
5 - Accusations

C. How did this person want to make me feel?

2 - Afraid

D. What did this person want me to do?

5 - Obey

E. How would I respond?

Letter 16

Hi, what's up? Me, not too much, just that I miss you. I know you might think I'm an asshole for all the stuff I did to you and I'm sorry. Well, I guess you know by now, I'm not coming back because of all the junk I did. But, I'll be going home in no time at all and I would like for us to get back together. If you don't mind having a boyfriend off campus. Because before I got kicked out, I wanted to get back with you before I left, but I didn't know I'd be leaving. I still love you and ain't anything going to change it. When I was going with *****, I could not take my mind off you. I know I messed up by letting you go and I might not get you back. But I'm asking you to give me one more chance. We could have a better relationship now that I'll be home. I could meet you on your outings. I'm really sorry for the stuff I did to you. Sorry! And I plan on making it up to you. So what do you think? I'll treat you right and I'm not going to do anything behind your back. Then when you leave we can live together. You are what I live for. So without you my soul is black and my heart is empty. It might sound like I'm trying to get over on you but I'm not. I mean everything I say. It comes from the heart. I cry just about every night hoping I could be with you. You're the best girl I ever had and I lost you. But I'm asking for one

more chance to be with you and treat you like a Queen should be treated. And a Queen is what you is. A Queen that I need in my life to keep me out of trouble and if you look back you can see I did not really start getting in trouble until I let you go. Please come back to me, I need you.

A. What was this person trying to do?

2 - Create a secret relationship

B. What tactic(s) was the groomer using?

2 - Insecurity
6 - Flattery

C. How did this person want to make me feel?

1 - Special
6 - Loved

D. What did this person want me to do?

8 - Be the "only one" in this person's life

E. How would I respond?

Letter 17

I just thought I'd tell you that you'll never find another person like me who loves with all of their heart. I guess I see now that you haven't noticed. It hurts so much inside. I want it to go away. Talk to me openly and honestly so I'll understand the most important question in my life, am I still an important person in your life? Please tell me because sometimes I don't know whether to stay or to go. You need to choose who you want to be with the most and be loyal to them. If other people aren't happy, then I guess they never did like you. I don't know what to do. Sometimes I feel you don't understand the real me. I try to let you find me, but it seems you never want to. Well, gotta cruise Keep in touch. Love lasts forever.

A. What was this person trying to do?

1 - Develop my trust

B. What tactic(s) was the groomer using?

2 - Insecurity

C. How did this person want to make me feel?

4 - Guilty

D. What did this person want me to do?

7 - Share my feelings

E. How would I respond?

Letter 18

You mean a lot to me. You are the only boy I want to be with. When you said we should start talking to other people, I thought I was going to die. I don't want you to go out with someone else. I don't know what I would do. It's all up to you. ***** and I had a long talk after school, and I told him how I feel about you and nothing was going to stop me from talking to you. The way you were acting last week, I thought you were just playing with my mind. If you knew how much I cared about you, you might change your mind. I can't stop thinking about what you said about being friends. I don't want you as a friend, I see you as a special friend. I would do anything to be with you and I mean that. Please write back. I need to hear an answer.

A. What was this person trying to do?

2 - Create a secret relationship

B. What tactic(s) was the groomer using?

1 - Jealousy and possessiveness
2 - Insecurity
8 - Bribery

C. How did this person want to make me feel?

4 - Guilty

D. What did this person want me to do?

8 - Be the "only one" in this person's life

E. How would I respond?

Letter 19

We can't let anyone break us apart. If we get into an argument or disagreement we will work it out. People here can't be trusted. Only trust me. I couldn't wait to ask you out so I did it on the phone. I didn't get to say all I wanted but I said the most important thing. But I still will ask you in your face and do it the right way. You mean a lot to me and we can't let anyone break us apart. I don't want to lose you for anything. I think I would kill myself if I lost you. You mean everything to me. Don't let people break us apart for anything.

A. What was this person trying to do?

1 - Develop my trust

B. What tactic(s) was the groomer using?

2 - Insecurity
9 - Control

C. How did this person want to make me feel?

6 - Loved

D. What did this person want me to do?

6 - Believe everything he or she says

E. How would I respond?

Letter 20

I was so happy to hear your voice on the phone last night. When I get home, if I see you I will give you something I've been wanting to give you for the longest time. Even though you said I could do something with a girl for one day, I won't because I only want you. I only want one girl and that's you. What would you do if I kissed you? Would you hit me or kiss me back? I was just wondering because I might just do it one day. You have to hurry up so we can go out to the movies sometimes. I hope I will be able to see you. We really do want to be with each other. I did something bad after I got off the phone, but it wasn't with a girl. I would never do anything to hurt you or do anything behind your back. You mean too much to me to let you go. I won't let anyone get in our relationship. It's hard for me to tell someone I love them. But I could tell you because I care about you, you care about me, and I could finally be open to someone I love a lot I mean every word I say to you from the bottom of my heart. I could go on forever telling you how much I want to be with you, but I won't because you already know how I feel about you.

A. What was this person trying to do?

   1 - Develop my trust

B. What tactic(s) was the groomer using?

   2 - Insecurity
   4 - Control
   8 - Bribery

C. How did this person want to make me feel?

   1 - Special
   6 - Loved

D. What did this person want me to do?

   6 - Believe everything he or she says

E. How would I respond?

Letter 21

I know a lot of guys like me but I don't like them. I do want to keep this low for awhile so I don't build a bad rep. You know what I'm sayin'. You seem like a nice person to me. I hope that one day you and I will be closer together. You look good and you know it. I understand that you want a fine babe like me, so don't get all choked up. You treat me right and you'll see what that brings you. Don't you dare let anyone read this letter.

P.S. Remember keep this LOW!

A. What was this person trying to do?

   2 - Create a secret relationship

B. What tactic(s) was the groomer using?

   6 - Flattery
   7 - Status

C. How did this person want to make me feel?

   1 - Special

D. What did this person want me to do?

   5 - Obey

E. How would I respond?

Letter 22

You are such a sweetheart! Wuz up? Well, with me there's not much going on if I must say. Don't you trust me in many ways? Do you think that if you and I ever did something together that I would tell someone?

I wouldn't dare try to tell anyone anything you tell me. I actually do believe in you too much to let you down. It's been about 2 1/2 months since I got a letter from you. And here is your answers to the questions okay, baby doll,

1. Do I still like you, of course I do. I like you more than just a friend.

2. ***** and I are just friends okay and nothing else.

3. Well, I think that you are a wonderful person and I do admire you for your sweetness. I think of you as an angel to me because I adore the things you do and the way you do them. I know that you are absolutely lovely and I really mean it when I say that you are worth the time.

4. If I had the chance of going out with you again, I would take the chance because you were and still is the best girl out of all my girls that I've had and I'm really serious about that also. Although we aren't going out, you always make me feel good and wanted.

You are just simply the sweetest. I hope that you're being treated fairly by *****. I wish that we had never broken up. Do you still like me like I do? I want our friendship to carry on like it's been going so far. By the way, do you still wanna go on the outing together? I just wouldn't want to miss that. I'll always be good to you because I care for you also sweetheart. Always stay the way you are just for me and keep young and beautiful okay baby cakes. You are on my mind. I'll call you baby cakes from now on if you don't mind! I don't know what I want for my birthday but anything will do okay baby cakes. 2 of us 2 gether and 4 ever. To my "crystal". Luv You. From your "diamond",

A. What was this person trying to do?

   2 - Create a secret relationship

B. What tactic(s) was the groomer using?

   6 - Flattery
   9 - Control

C. How did this person want to make me feel?

   1 - Special
   6 - Loved

D. What did this person want me to do?

   7 - Share my feelings

E. How would I respond?

Letter 23

How are you doing. I'm fine. Could be better. It feels good to talk to you on the phone. Maybe it will be better when we talk face to face. It's not that I'm using *****, it's just that I can talk to my friends if I want to. I like her, yes. She's leaving and its going to be hard for her to leave because she says she likes me a lot But I can't tell if she does or not. I've talked to you for two days. I think you're a very nice person and you and me will become good friends or more. I can't tell how things are going to be. I can tell you one thing, I'm not a player. It's that a lot of these girls are like you. They like what they see and I can't help that, right? There's guys that think you're hot. I do. I just don't want other guys trying to start a relationship with you just to use you. I won't. If someone gets to start a relationship with you, I won't fight them or anything. I just want them to treat you well. You deserve that. I know I would treat you fine. See you later, I have to get some sleep. Write back.

A. What was this person trying to do?

   1 - Develop my trust

B. What tactic(s) was the groomer using?

   6 - Flattery
   7 - Status

C. How did this person want to make me feel?

   1 - Special

D. What did this person want me to do?

   6 - Believe everything he or she says

E. How would I respond?

Letter 24

Smile, laugh and think about it!! Stopping by to say a word or two. Hi! How are ya sweet thing? I'm doing okay I guess. Why don't you understand me at times? I wanted to talk to you after school but you left because of *****. We are not talking, in fact she's going out with this ***** guy and I was only signing her book. By the way I'm sorry if I did something that might have gotten you upset. I was unable to use the phone and I also couldn't go to the field house because of this ***** girl. Anyways, you may feel as if I only want one thing from you but that's totally untrue. If you feel as if I'm leading you on, maybe I shouldn't call or bother you then because I don't want to be guilty of anything. It's all up to you to decide what you wanna do. Maybe I'm getting in your way or something? Am I or am I not? I do like you a lot even though we're not going out. If I didn't would I waste my 5 minutes of phone call on you? Would I call you when there's a lot more girls that I could be calling or would I even talk to you? I'm not too good for you at all because there's no such thing. *****, please believe me I do care and like you and I wouldn't be wasting my time if I didn't. I know what you mean and I do understand too but I sometimes wonder where should I start. I don't want you to get in a position where you'll feel all confused because I want you to be happy. Think about it okay!! Gots to go for now and I'll see ya later. Love you lots!

A. What was this person trying to do?

   1 - Develop my trust

B. What tactic(s) was the groomer using?

   6 - Flattery
   7 - Status

C. How did this person want to make me feel?

   1 - Special

D. What did this person want me to do?

   6 - Believe everything he or she says

E. How would I respond?

Letter 25

What you said earlier at the picnic keeps repeating itself over and over in my mind. About love, kids and us. Please believe me. It's not you at all. It's me. Number one. My self esteem ain't the best, it's very low. Two, I'm not really positive when a guy loves me for me or for some other reason. Three, I'm scared. Because every other male liked me for sex, popularity, looks or something else.

I do love you, *****. I love every moment we spend together even if it is when I get annoyed with you. I still love you. I just hate not being able to touch you. No hand-holding, no hugging, no kissing, no nothing, zip. That's why your kiss surprised me so much and every time you touch me I feel warm inside and when I'm with you I feel like it is for real. You really love me for me and there was no other guys before who hurt me, there's only you. Then when you leave I feel insecure again and I feel like crying because I'm scared you'll leave me for someone else. And hurt me again. I do want to have a child. A boy. And it's painful to know that there's a 99% chance I can't because of miscarriages and other reasons. You tripped me out when you said lets leave and go do that. I swear you were kidding. When I think someone's serious I'll usually go do it. But no one here is usually serious. I wanted to believe you were serious. I would of gone in a heartbeat if I thought you were.

But like I said I want someone who loves me enough to stay with me when I do become pregnant. I also want the love so when I look into that child's eyes I can see the love that we share to make that child. So, it won't hurt to look at it. To know the father loves me and shares that responsibility of the child with me. I love you so much and I want you to know that. There really isn't really any way you can prove that you love me except with love, and time. Hopefully time will go fast right? Maybe it will maybe it won't. All I know is you need to be patient. And the day that I am 100 percent sure that our relationship is secure is... well, you'll know.

That's the first time you ever told me how much you loved me so I could hear it. Not write it but told me. And I felt so good inside. Like when you touch me. Hopefully, soon time will come for us to be together for a long, long time. Maybe forever. I want you to remember that okay? I love you.

A. What was this person trying to do?

1 - Develop my trust

B. What tactic(s) was the groomer using?

2 - Insecurity
7 - Status
9 - Control

C. How did this person want to make me feel?

7- This person needs me to be happy and successful

D. What did this person want me to do?

8 - Be the "only one" in this person's life

E. How would I respond?

Letter 26

What's up my love? I have been thinking about you night and day. I've been thinking about how much I love you which is a lot. Some other things I've been thinking about is when I first saw you and when I held you in my arms in back of the school. I miss you so much. I can't wait to see you again. There's a lot of things I love about you. You're smart, you have a sweet personality and you are very pretty. You are very special to me. Just thinking about you makes me happy. I really

want to be there for you. You are too sweet to be taken advantage of and treated bad. And I don't want that to happen. I do like to do it, but, we are going to take it nice slow. You know what I'm saying. Some time I will show you how much I love you, but not right now. Gotta go.

A. What was this person trying to do?

1 - Develop my trust

B. What tactic(s) was the groomer using?

6 - Flattery

C. How did this person want to make me feel?

1 - Special
6 - Loved

D. What did this person want me to do?

6 - Believe everything he or she says

E. How would I respond?

Letter 27

I'm just thinking about you and how pretty you are. I really like you a lot. I feel like asking you out but that would have been going too fast. I don't want to do anything to get you in trouble. Do you want to start talking? If we start talking, we can't be talking for 8 months and that's all if you know what I mean. You're all I think about and I'm not saying that just to make you like me more. I'm writing this to let you know how I feel about you, and I mean every word I say to you. I was telling ********** about how I feel about you and he said he was going to start talking to you because he likes you too. But, I'm not going to let him get in my way of talking to you. He's not for you. He may do something to hurt you and I won't. He plays on all of the girls he has ever gone out with. Stay away from him. You are very pretty and I mean that. If we were going out, I would want you to know I would never do anything to hurt you.

A. What was this person trying to do?

   1 - Develop my trust

B. What tactic(s) was the groomer using?

   6 - Flattery

C. How did this person want to make me feel?

   1 - Special

D. What did this person want me to do?

   6 - Believe everything he or she says

E. How would I respond?

Letter 28

Hey sweetness, how are ya? Me, okay I guess. I had a great day yesterday with you. That's the way I want you to treat me. Like a good friend. So, we're still going out, aren't we? I hope so. I was so happy that you asked me out. I've wanted you to do that for the longest time. Oh! Yesterday, did ***** find out what we did after school? I thought I was busted because of them. It was really strange when you said, "If I have sex with you, I'll have to be with you forever." Why did you say that? Do you want to do that so we can be together forever? That would be so great, but your parents suck. They won't give us another chance. I hope this time our relationship lasts, even if they don't like it. Sorry for leaving yesterday after school. I wish I could have stayed with you forever, but you know those stupid rules. This is so great. We're together still after all the problems in the past. Now we have to look at the present and deal with it in a positive way so we can be together. There's one thing I got to ask of you - please, whatever you do, don't hurt me. I love you too much to be hurt by you. That means if you see me in the hall, don't just walk by me. Another

thing, will you please not write ***** and ***** anymore? If they ask you why you don't write them, say, "I don't have time." I'm not saying you can't talk to them. You can, that's fine, but if you see me, I'd appreciate it if you'd talk to me. Well, later up! Love always.

A. What was this person trying to do?

   1 - Develop my trust

B. What tactic(s) was the groomer using?

   2 - Insecurity
   9 - Control

C. How did this person want to make me feel?

   6 - Loved

D. What did this person want me to do?

   8 - Be the "only one" in this person's life

E. How would I respond?

Letter 29

Hi honey. How are you. When I said I would give you something special, I take that back. I don't want you to think anything about that. I want you to do good cause hopefully you'd feel good and that would make me feel good. Speaking of good asses, you got a nice one yourself. I like you for what you are not what you can give. It's just that sometimes when I'm around you I feel like doing this and that. I want to get closer and stuff and don't do all this negative stuff. Then nature can take its time. Let's get closer but don't go too far. I want you badly. But I will wait if I have to. I have other stuff to say but I don't want to write it down.

A. What was this person trying to do?

   1 - Develop my trust

B. What tactic(s) was the groomer using?

6 - Flattery
8 - Bribery

C. How did this person want to make me feel?

1 - Special

D. What did this person want me to do?

6 - Believe everything he or she says

E. How would I respond?

Letter 30

What's Up?

How are you doin' sweetheart? Myself, thinking about you mostly. I wish I could be with you so much. I called you back last night and your mom answered the phone and she told me that I couldn't call you anymore because I was too old to talk to you. I know you don't like that any more than I do but I promise you we will work around that. Because I like you too much and no matter what anybody says, I will always be there for you. Nobody can keep us apart. I want you to be my girl. I want to ask you face to face so you can see for yourself how serious I am. I love you and I want you to be happy. You deserve a lot of tender lovin' care, and I want to be the one to give it to you. That's from the bottom of my heart.

A. What was this person trying to do?

1 - Develop my trust

B. What tactic(s) was the groomer using?

9 - Control

C. How did this person want to make me feel?

1 - Special
6 - Loved

D. What did this person want me to do?

6 - Believe everything he or she says

E. How would I respond?

Letter 31

I know you are coming back from the lake tomorrow. So I will call you and see how you are doing and to talk about our relationship. We do make a good couple if you ask me. I just got me a Michael Jordan jump suit. I was going to try and get you one, but I don't have any money right now. But I get paid 60 dollars Friday if it all works out. My parents will be watching how I spend it so I'll have to think of something. I have fallen in love with you and I mean that. I can't wait to see you because I have something for you and I have to do something. It's a surprise. And I'm not going to tell, I will just wait for the right time. I hope you will like it, I know you will. I've been in the house all day watching TV and being bored. Have you told ***** about us? I know if you tell her or anybody else they would be happy for you. Because a lot of people said we make a good couple and that's the truth. I won't let you get away from me anymore cause I love you and yes I do love you. I can't wait till you see your surprise!

A. What was this person trying to do?

1 - Develop my trust

B. What tactic(s) was the groomer using?

8 - Bribery

C. How did this person want to make me feel?

1 - Special

D. What did this person want me to do?

6 - Believe everything he or she says

E. How would I respond?

Letter 32

Did you get the tape I made for you. I mixed it myself. All of the songs on there remind me of you. I especially like the one that says I can't wait 2 get 2 school each day, and wait for you to pass my way, and the bells start to ring, an angel starts 2 say, Hey that's the girl for you, so what are you gonna do, hey little girl I love you. All I do is think of you day and night that's all I do. I can't get you off my mind. Think about you all the time, all the time girl. I've begun 2 take the long way home just so I can be alone 2 think of how 2 say my heart is here to stay.

If I could do it I'd buy you everything you wanted. Remember that sweater at the mall. That would look so good on you baby. Someday I'll buy it or steal it if I have to. You mean the world to me and I want to show you how much. Well it's late and I'd better get to bed.

P.S. If you still want pictures just let me know.

A. What was this person trying to do?

   1 - Develop my trust

B. What tactic(s) was the groomer using?

   8 - Bribery

C. How did this person want to make me feel?

   1 - Special

D. What did this person want me to do?

   6 - Believe everything he or she says

E. How would I respond?

Letter 33

I'm just sitting in bed thinking about our relationship. I feel that we are going to get closer and closer fast. I wish I could give you something before I leave if you know what I mean. I will miss you and I will be thinking about you every second of the day. I care about you in many different ways, and I mean that from the bottom of my heart. I wish I could see you right now, and tell you how

much I want and need you. I don't want to lose you for anything. We can't be lettin' other people try to keep us from getting closer. We are made for each other. The song that makes me think about our relationship is One More Try. It's all about us that's why I like it. I won't do anything to hurt you and I won't mess with any girls because I want to be with one person. And that's you. Trust me. You don't do anything bad, if you know what I mean. I will miss you a lot. I love you in many ways.

A. What was this person trying to do?

   1 - Develop my trust

B. What tactic(s) was the groomer using?

   2 - Insecurity
   9 - Control

C. How did this person want to make me feel?

   1 - Special
   6 - Loved

D. What did this person want me to do?

   6 - Believe everything he or she says

E. How would I respond?

Letter 34

I'm just chillin out with the home boyz, and staying out of trouble, as usual. If only I could see you now and show you how much I miss you. I keep calling everyday, but someone is always on the phone. I've been going to the mall and I'm going to a party Friday. And, I won't do anything wrong (such as girls). I wish I had a picture of you so I could look at you and hold it close to my heart. I keep thinking about what I said to you on the phone, about how I wasn't going to mess with any girls. Well, I haven't. So that means you have to do the same thing. I'm not saying you're not, but, you know what I'm saying. I'm not letting you get away from me anymore. I'm in love with you. And I'll be good to you. Remember that.

A. What was this person trying to do?

   1 - Develop my trust

B. What tactic(s) was the groomer using?

   9 - Control

C. How did this person want to make me feel?

   1 - Special

D. What did this person want me to do?

   6 - Believe everything he or she says

E. How would I respond?

Letter 35

I'm doing nothing but watching TV and doing homework. Just thinking about you, I start smiling because you mean a lot to me. Now that I have fallen in love with you. I can't wait to see you because I'm going to ask you out right then and there. We have to be honest with each other all the time. Don't ever run away because you will just get in a lot of trouble. But if you want to sneak out and see me, that's OK, but don't get caught. I wish I could see you right now. The way I see it, you want to be with me, and I want to be with you. That says we are made for each other. You are more important than anything in my life. So remember that. You're mine from here on. If you want to sneak out just tell me when so I can be outside. We might get caught if we go in the house. Love.

A. What was this person trying to do?

   2 - Create a secret relationship

B. What tactic(s) was the groomer using?

   9 - Control

C. How did this person want to make me feel?

   6 - Loved

D. What did this person want me to do?

   9 - Leave without permission

E. How would I respond?

Letter 36

You mean a lot to me in so many ways. I hope you like the pictures. I'm love sick not seeing you. When I saw you in church, I wanted to give you a big hug and kiss. That new girl kept looking at me like she likes me. But don't worry. If only you were here right now, I'd give you something you'd never forget. Are you thinking about me right now, because I just can't stop thinking about you and how pretty you are. I'm going to kick *****'s ass if he doesn't quit hitting on you. Do you like him? I don't want him to come between us. I think about you all the time.

A. What was this person trying to do?

   1 - Develop my trust

B. What tactic(s) was the groomer using?

   6 - Flattery
   7 - Status

C. How did this person want to make me feel?

   1 - Special
   6 - Loved

D. What did this person want me to do?

   6 - Believe everything he or she says

E. How would I respond?

Letter 37

I'm so happy because I will be able to see you tomorrow. Did you miss me, because

I missed you. I know we've only known each other for five days, but I want to treat you right. You're the first girl I've ever fallen in love with so fast. We need to get together to talk about our relationship. See if I can come over one day. I know you'll be able to come over here but your ***** are different. You should start going to the Field House more so we can see each other more. I made a song about you and me. It's good, I'll let you hear it one day. As soon as I see you, I'm going to ask you out because I can't wait anymore. When are you going to give me a picture of you? I don't care if you just woke up or look dead, just give me one. I love you so much, and I know you will love me if you just give me a chance. Closer, closer, closer, closer.

A. What was this person trying to do?

> **1 - Develop my trust**

B. What tactic(s) was the groomer using?

> **9 - Control**

C. How did this person want to make me feel?

> **1 - Special**

D. What did this person want me to do?

> **6 - Believe everything he or she says**

E. How would I respond?

Letter 38

I know that we've only been talking for two days, but I want to tell you how fine I think you are. You make me feel like no one else ever has in my life. Can you meet me behind the Field House tonight. I just want to talk to you in private with no one else around so I can tell you how I really feel. I won't do anything else, I promise. You will know that I can be trusted when you get to know me better. I would never hurt you or anything like that. Let me know if you can meet me.

A. What was this person trying to do?

> **1 - Develop my trust**

B. What tactic(s) was the groomer using?

> **6 - Flattery**

C. How did this person want to make me feel?

> **1 - Special**

D. What did this person want me to do?

> **6 - Believe everything he or she says**

E. How would I respond?

Letter 39

What's up? Not much this way. Just chillin' out at work writing you this note. So you and ***** gonna start goin' out? I was just wondering because if you weren't I'd like to get with you. I've always had this thing about fine girls. You and me would be a great couple. Well, anyway, what has ***** been saying about me? She's alright but I don't think I would go out with her. She's not fine enough for me. Anyway, you haven't told me anything about you. The only thing I know is that you are from *****. Well, think about you and me getting together. Let's just keep you and me a secret, OK?

P.S. why don't you call me!

A. What was this person trying to do?

> **2 - Create a secret relationship**

B. What tactic(s) was the groomer using?

> **6 - Flattery**
> **7 - Status**

C. How did this person want to make me feel?

> **1 - Special**
> **6 - Loved**

D. What did this person want me to do?

6 - Believe everything he or she says

E. How would I respond?

Letter 40

I tried to call you so many times yesterday. Every time I call you someone is always on it. I'll give you some pictures of me so you can look at them before you go to bed. Don't play me like a sucker again, that pisses me off. Plus I won't let you because I want you more than anyone does.

A. What was this person trying to do?

1 - Develop my trust

B. What tactic(s) was the groomer using?

4 - Intimidation
9 - Control

C. How did this person want to make me feel?

1 - Special

D. What did this person want me to do?

8 - Be the "only one" in this person's life

E. How would I respond?

Letter 41

I went over to my friends house this morning to see if he was going to buy the speakers still. I lowered the price to 25 dollars. It's hard for me to stay out of trouble. We bought half a stick of dynamite yesterday, from some drunk man. How much do you have left on daily, so we can go out. It's 12:15 a.m. right now and we just got through egging cars and houses. I didn't get caught so don't worry about it. I can't sleep because it's too hot and I'm thinking about you. Do you think I could come over to your house one day or you could come over to mine? I want

to be with you for a long time. Do you want to be with me for a long time? Maybe you could help me stay out of trouble. You would be so good for me. Just remember I want you and no one else.

A. What was this person trying to do?

1 - Develop my trust

B. What tactic(s) was the groomer using?

9 - Control
7 - Status

C. How did this person want to make me feel?

2 - Afraid

D. What did this person want me to do?

6 - Believe everything he or she says

E. How would I respond?

Letter 42

What's up. I'm just sitting on the bed thinking about what I should do to you the next time I see you. I miss you so much and I feel like I'm going to die if I don't see you. Tell me that we have gotten real close. I feel like I've known you forever. I collect the "Love Is" cartoons and I have certain ones for you. I know you would like them. I was just thinking about what you would do if I tried to kiss you. What would you do if I tried something else. Not saying I will, just wondering, but I'd like to. Think about it.

A. What was this person trying to do?

1 - Develop my trust

B. What tactic(s) was the groomer using?

2 - Insecurity
9 - Control

C. How did this person want to make me feel?

1 - Special

D. What did this person want me to do?

7 - Share my feelings

E. How would I respond?

Letter 43

A lot of people are happy that we're talking and I am very happy. I'm sorry that I haven't been spending a lot of time with you, because of *****. I'll tell her somehow that I don't want to talk to her anymore. It will be hard because she likes me a lot, but I have to tell her, because I want to talk to one person and that's you. I just don't want to hurt anyone that's all. That's the type of guy I am. You're all I think about. I think about you every second of the day. I am real sorry. When you were mad at me, I didn't know what to do because you wouldn't talk to me. And then I saw you talking with *****, and I thought you were talking. I don't want to lose you to anybody else. So are we still talking or can I ask you out? We are a fine couple together, no doubt about it. A lot of people have told me that. You are sweet and so sexy too.

A. What was this person trying to do?

1 - Develop my trust

B. What tactic(s) was the groomer using?

1 - Jealousy and possessiveness
6 - Flattery
7 - Status

C. How did this person want to make me feel?

1 - Special

D. What did this person want me to do?

6 - Believe everything he or she says

E. How would I respond?

Letter 44

I'm just sitting in bed thinking about all the stuff we talked about over the phone. I know we haven't known each other that long, but since we have talked for 2 days, it seems like I know you like the back of my hand. I really like you a lot and I mean that from the bottom of my heart. I'm not like *****, trying to just get some, if you know what I mean. I wanted to talk to you when you first got here, but I didn't know how. I wish we were talking right now. But you're still with *****. Are you going to tell him that you don't want to talk anymore? If you do, we can't start seeing each other right away, because he'll know something is up. Would you start talking with me if I asked you? You're all I think about now. I'm always thinking about things we could do, if you know what I mean.

P.S. Don't show this to anyone, O.K.

A. What was this person trying to do?

1 - Develop my trust

B. What tactic(s) was the groomer using?

2 - Insecurity
9 - Control

C. How did this person want to make me feel?

1 - Special

D. What did this person want me to do?

7 - Share my feelings

E. How would I respond?

Letter 45

Hey, hi. Well, I'm sorry I didn't write until now, but I was real busy with senior homework. You understand, don't ya? Well, I can't wait till we're able to spend some real time together. You know what I'm sayin' too!

But anyways, you're gonna have a baby by me once I leave from here, so be prepared! I can't wait to rescue another kiss from you! *****, I believe we could possibly turn out to be somethin' special. You know what I'm sayin'. Well honey, I must go now, ok!

I'll call you before I bust a move to the game!

Love = Me

A. What was this person trying to do?

1 - Develop my trust

B. What tactic(s) was the groomer using?

9 - Control

C. How did this person want to make me feel?

1 - Special

D. What did this person want me to do?

6 - Believe everything he or she says

E. How would I respond?

Letter 46

What's up? I'm just sitting in the basement thinking about you, and how long we've been talking. I'm glad we are, because I like you a lot. ***** wants me to ask you out, but I told her that that would be rushing it too fast. I want to, but as I said it would be rushing it. ***** really wants to go out with me, but I don't know how to say NO, but I will somehow. That's why you see me with her, because of the problems we had together. She wants to talk about them. That's all, we're just talking. If I asked you out would you say "Yes," "No," or "Why." You can't be getting into trouble and losing your privileges because I need to talk to you. I think if we went out together we would last a long time if we don't let other people or problems break

us apart. Sometimes I can't sleep at night because I think about you and other relationships I've had and what I would do to you. But mostly I think about what we could do together. We would be fine together. When you told me about what happened to you back home, I couldn't stop thinking why someone would want to beat you. I hate hearing things like that, I want you to know I would never do anything to hurt you.

A. What was this person trying to do?

1 - Develop my trust

B. What tactic(s) was the groomer using?

7 - Status
9 - Control

C. How did this person want to make me feel?

3 - Safe

D. What did this person want me to do?

7 - Share my feelings

E. How would I respond?

Letter 47

What's down? Nothing here, but the earth that has a sweet and special young lady on it named *****! Well, I'm just laying here listening to Boys to Men, "Please Don't Go Away From Me" and thinking about the other night we expressed some of our feelings for each other in a physical way! That kept me warm and made me feel relaxed. And I felt so good with you lying in my arms, as I played with your hair and ran my hands across your ever so soft body! But, the main part I keep in my mind is when I was about to go and you asked for a hug good-bye. And I was kneeling on the bed, and as I pulled you closer to me, the light from the windows behind me was shining on your beautiful eyes that seemed to be sparkling with happiness as I pulled you even closer and then kissed your soft lips! It was from that point on since I feel that you do like me!!

I'm glad that you let me know your feelings for me in your letters that you write to me. Because some girls like you, and they never tell you nothing. So, then you don't know if they really care for you or not. So, keep letting me know how you feel about me, okay?

Everything has just been going so well between us. I hope it will last a long time. but, I also know we will have our bad times. But, if we care for each other enough, we will get over all of the bad things. So, if you ever feel mad at me, or you are upset about something, just let me know what's up! Because I would really want to know what I did wrong so that I could correct my mistake!

Well, I just want you to know that I do care for you, and I know you are a really nice person. So, now I am about to go, so write back as soon as possible and make it good!

P.S. I am gonna call you Twinkles.

A. What was this person trying to do?

   1 - Develop my trust

B. What tactic(s) was the groomer using?

   6 - Flattery
   9 - Control

C. How did this person want to make me feel?

   1 - Special

D. What did this person want me to do?

   7 - Share my feelings

E. How would I respond?

Letter 48

Hey Sweet thang. What's down. Not much here. Just got done with my homework. You know I felt like grabbing you and just start making out right there in that little room. But I didn't cause there were too many people around. So what I'm saying is that we need to be alone. Meet me after school today and we'll go somewhere and then I can get my kiss.

I think you should start doing better. And then you can come with me to the movies. Or not with me but meet me at the movie theater. You know what I mean.

Well, I don't know what else to write cause I'm having a bad day. But I love you. And if you ever need a shoulder to lean on or just a hug and someone to talk to, I'll be there when you need me. And yes, I know the situation is sneaky but who cares. I'll stay with you anyway, no matter what. You can also hold me whenever you want, any time. And when I look at you I say to myself, don't let this one get away. But I love you very much.

A friend and secret love,

Don't let no one see this letter, it's our secret.

A. What was this person trying to do?

   2 - Create a secret relationship

B. What tactic(s) was the groomer using?

   9 - Control

C. How did this person want to make me feel?

   1 - Special

D. What did this person want me to do?

   8 - Be the "only one" in this person's life

E. How would I respond?

Letter 49

Hey good lookin'! What's up? I was really excited talking to you on the phone tonight. I haven't talked to you in a long time. I couldn't believe we kissed right where we did today. We could have gotten busted big time. I think we better be more careful in the future, like when there's no one around, or you're walking me to the field house 5th period, or after school down by the food services door. I just don't want to get busted because if I do, I don't know what my teachers will say to me. How come you wouldn't take your picture with me at Homecoming? I really want some more pictures of you, as many as ***** has of you. I also would really like a picture of you and me together. I think your house should have a party and you said your parents aren't that strict, so maybe we could get busy. I don't know why I've been acting so strange lately, but I have been wanting sex put it that way. Well what do you think about that. Well I better break so I can go to sleep and dream about you. I wish I could dream about you and remember it, but I can't. How do I know you care and love me if you never tell me?

A. What was this person trying to do?

2 - Create a secret relationship

B. What tactic(s) was the groomer using?

6 - Flattery
9 - Control

C. How did this person want to make me feel?

1 - Special

D. What did this person want me to do?

7 - Share my feelings

E. How would I respond?

Letter 50

For these gorgeous eyes of yours only!

What's kickin' hon? Just peeking to say a word or two. I'm badly in need of enjoying the most happiest moments with you alone. The fun and pleasure begins with what you have and therefore it's quite out of reach. There's nothing I'd like to do more than kissing your gentle lips and slightly pulling your tongue with compassion.

Most likely I'd want to touch you all over and see if you're really ticklish. I want to put my legs between your thighs and do the wild thing.

Loneliness won't leave me alone and I feel like being with you every second of the day having fun and also playing with your belly button your face is so smooth which wants to make me put my arms around you and run my fingers through your hair. I'd like to feel what's in between your legs and give to you what you might of never felt before. I want to make you feel the heat all over your body and I also want to make you scream as if you were badly in pain. My mind is on you every time and if I could fly with somebody, that someone would be you. I'll give you more than you want and can take. If only this would come true. I don't want to go on without your love and beauty. I'll be waiting for your call anytime. There's a job that has to be done and I really want to work on your body.

I do love and want you. The next time I ever kiss you, there will be a difference in it. So keep cute just for me okay. Love ya all the time. I can't wait too long. To my sweetness. You're my lover girl!

A. What was this person trying to do?

2 - Create a secret relationship

B. What tactic(s) was the groomer using?

2 - Insecurity
6 - Flattery
9 - Control

C. How did this person want to make me feel?

5 - Sexually aroused

D. What did this person want me to do?

2 - Have sex

E. How would I respond?

Letter 51

You know you said you will do anything for me. Let me see what you can do. Don't show a single soul this letter especially not *****. Cause I don't want her giving you a bunch of shit, which she will. Please don't show anyone, please. And at AA I will get the kiss I never had the chance to get. You will have your socks knocked off by me. And don't go out with *****. He's going to hurt you more and I don't want to see you get hurt. I think all he thinks about sex. You need a man of sensitivity and that's me. Don't think I couldn't get loose around you, because I could. I could make you feel real good if I got the chance. See you later, gotta go.

A. What was this person trying to do?

2 - Create a secret relationship

B. What tactic(s) was the groomer using?

9 - Control

C. How did this person want to make me feel?

1 - Special

D. What did this person want me to do?

5 - Obey

E. How would I respond?

Letter 52

If you get in trouble doing anything wrong and I hear about it, you will deal with me. I don't want to do anything with any other girl except you. I'm the only one who is right for you. So don't play on me, OK. You wouldn't want to see me mad. Our relationship is working out real fine right now and we're getting closer and closer. Don't mess it up. We have real feelings for one another. Just do what I say and everything will be alright.

A. What was this person trying to do?

1 - Develop my trust

B. What tactic(s) was the groomer using?

4 - Intimidation
5 - Accusations
9 - Control

C. How did this person want to make me feel?

2 - Afraid

D. What did this person want me to do?

5 - Obey

E. How would I respond?

Letter 53

I didn't say you did anything. But just tell me or not if you did anything with *****. If you want him, just go out with him. I'll get over it. It's not like you would really care anyway. You can't say that I've did anything to ***** cause I didn't. You can believe any damned person you want to. I didn't do nothin to her. ***** even came up to me and said some things about you and him, and what you did. Don't do this to me, even when I hear this stuff, it hurts my feelings. No, that's not all I want either and who ever you been hearing this from is lying or something. I guess it's no big deal. I just don't think I'm really your type or good enough for you. I'm screwing too many things up. I'm not worth it. So let me know if you want to stop our relationship, I'll try to understand. I probably deserve it anyway. The way I treat you, I'm not doing it the way I'm supposed to. I guess I was wrong. I'm sorry for treating you the way I did.

A. What was this person trying to do?

   1 - Develop my trust

B. What tactic(s) was the groomer using?

   2 - Insecurity
   5 - Accusations

C. How did this person want to make me feel?

   4 - Guilty

D. What did this person want me to do?

   4 - Apologize

E. How would I respond?

Letter 54

What's going on? Thanks for coming to my football game. I didn't know you were gonna come. I would have pulled up my shirt but then I thought I would look dumb pulling up my shirt. I would have given you some pictures of me but I can't find them anywhere. I have some coming on the way. Another thing, I sacrifice myself staying up all late and things, just to write you something. What do you do in return? I have some ideas. I'll tell you if you want to know. Another thing, I'm sorry for overreacting. I shouldn't have done that. I was really mad. And when I get mad I don't know what I'll do. Thanks for putting up with it. Why are you hitting on ***** for? I mean, you can talk to whoever you want but doing something else is another thing. Don't play around on

me. I don't like it. I was wondering if you get mad if I write to ***** or not. She asked me to write her. I hope you're doing OK. Well, I'll write more later.

A. What was this person trying to do?

   1 - Develop my trust

B. What tactic(s) was the groomer using?

   1 - Jealousy and possessiveness
   4 - Intimidation

C. How did this person want to make me feel?

   2 - Afraid

D. What did this person want me to do?

   5 - Obey

E. How would I respond?

Letter 55

So what's up Sweet Cakes. Not much here, just chillin' in English reading this boring story. So what's going on with us. Don't say you don't know, because I notice a lot of guys like you. I don't want to be sharing a girl. I want you to know that I do like you and I wouldn't mind getting to know you a lot better. There's probably a lot that goes around about me that you hear, but I hope you don't believe it. If there is anything that you do believe or are curious about, then feel free to ask me and I swear I will tell you the honest truth. You seem like a very nice person who would be a good friend also. (You look great too!!) If you can call me, call. So when you get a chance to tell me if we could get together let me know. Don't believe everything you hear about me unless you ask me if it's true. We'd be a good couple.

A. What was this person trying to do?

   1 - Develop my trust

B. What tactic(s) was the groomer using?

1 - Jealousy and possessiveness
5 - Accusations
6 - Flattery

C. How did this person want to make me feel?

1 - Special

D. What did this person want me to do?

6 - Believe everything he or she says

E. How would I respond?

D. What did this person want me to do?

5 - Obey

E. How would I respond?

Letter 56

How are you doin'? Myself, I'm not so doing too good, especially after I heard a few things about you from *****. Tomorrow ***** is supposed to be telling me some things about you. What kind of girl are you anyway. Your past isn't very good. If there is something you need to tell me, please do. I know that we haven't gone out yet, but I don't want to lose you. I have already decided that I want you and nobody else. And I hope you feel the same way. I don't want to hear a bunch of stuff about you from someone else. It makes me so mad, I don't know what I will do. I want to kick somebody's ass when I hear things about you. You need to be honest with me and let me know the truth. If you can, please try and call me tomorrow. I love you a lot, keep that in mind.

A. What was this person trying to do?

1 - Develop my trust

B. What tactic(s) was the groomer using?

4 - Intimidation
5 - Accusations
9 - Control

C. How did this person want to make me feel?

4 - Guilty

Letters for
Transparencies

Letter 1

Hello cute thing, I thought I'd write because you've written so much in the past and I've not written to you in a while. By the way, don't think that I wrote back to ***** okay. The world is for both you and I together and no one in between. You don't have to wonder just look into my eyes and my friendship will be right with you. I'm not cheating on you and I want you to understand that even though we don't get together much, I really do "love" you. I want just the two of us to hold on the precious moments and you are truly the water of my heart and river.

Whenever you tell me that you're crying, I feel that I'm doing something to hurt you and I feel so guilty "but why"? Your voice is like an angel to me and you're the reason why this boy wants to carry on. I've been living on the sweet things you've said and I don't want to hide it. You are the beautiful picture that I've got in my head and what is stopping us from being alone, I don't know. If I'm the one you love, do you trust me? If I didn't care about you, I would have chosen another girl but I really want you always. Let's not let this dream pass us by and let's talk to each other at school more often. You are for me and I'm for you so let's take part in what we want to give to each other.

I really don't want you to care so much about me and write so much until your fingers are sore okay "honey"! Take your time gently and remember that I love you because I'm doing this for you and all for love. You're in my mind. Keep "pretty", "sweet", "tender", "warm" and compassionate always. It's not always easy to be a friend but I'm your true friend and "I know what you need"! Please excuse my writing. I love you girl! From none other than yours truly,

A. What was this person trying to do?

B. What tactic(s) was the groomer using?

C. How did this person want to make me feel?

D. What did this person want me to do?

E. How would I respond?

Letter 2

I want you to know just because we got in trouble doesn't mean we can't still go out together. We just have to be more careful, that's all. If we keep everything a secret then no one will find out about what we do. Right?

I don't want us to part because it's stupid and it won't solve any-thing. You mean a lot to me in so many different ways. I love you. Don't let people put things in your head, if you know who I mean. I won't let you go. Don't worry about getting caught, OK? We need to stay together.

A. What was this person trying to do?

B. What tactic(s) was the groomer using?

C. How did this person want to make me feel?

D. What did this person want me to do?

E. How would I respond?

Letter 3

How are those people treating my sweetheart. I hope with some respect! I'm glad that you finally got around to writing me. I want you to know that I like you a lot too and like yourself I think of you a lot and wish that I could be with you 24/7. But it gets greater later when you finally get adjusted to this place (I hope soon) we will be spending a lot of time together. There's a lot of rules but I know the way around them. The main thing is that you just tell me about things and don't tell no one about us. I promise you that we will have some good times. Don't let the teachers see you writing letters. Write in private!

I forgive you for lying about your age. Just as long as you learned from it. Always keep me in your heart because you will always be in mine. And I want to keep you happy because that is the kind of respect I give to a girlfriend of mine. And you will be my girl sooner or later but, we both are going to take it nice and slow. If that is OK with you.

I have been thinking about you a lot and one of the things is that if you get mad or have an argument again and you run again. I don't want that to happen because you are really special to me and I don't want to lose you. Please try to call me. I have been trying to call you but nobody ever answer the phone.

P.S. You are pretty sexy yourself and you do know how to kiss real good. I want to see a picture of you baby whenever we see each other again. Don't worry about getting scared off by all the rules. But don't say anything to anyone, it's our secret baby.

A. What was this person trying to do?

B. What tactic(s) was the groomer using?

C. How did this person want to make me feel?

D. What did this person want me to do?

E. How would I respond?

Letter 4

I'm in bed thinking about you. We are not going to break up because of what happened. Because I love you and you love me. Please don't run away because it will make things worse and I don't want to see you get hurt or lose you. Don't change your story. We only talked, then did heavy kissing and I started to fall asleep. Don't change your story for nothing, because if your story is different from mine I can get sent away. I don't want to lose you for anything and I want us to be together for a long time. Even after we graduate, so please don't do anything wrong like yell at them or run away. I don't know what I would do if you left me. If have to leave I will come see you and take you with me where ever I go. You have changed my life a lot in so many special ways. If I can take it here, you can too. So don't think you can't. Love,

A. What was this person trying to do?

B. What tactic(s) was the groomer using?

C. How did this person want to make me feel?

D. What did this person want me to do?

E. How would I respond?

Letter 5

What's up chick? I really don't know about what we were talking about after school yesterday. I wouldn't mind, but you know what will happen if we do. How are we supposed to live? I sure couldn't get a job!! What made you decide to leave anyway? Baby, I would love nothing more than to be with you. The problem is if it would be the best thing for us. Is it really what we want to do? You do mean a lot to me, and I hope you know that.

If we do go, how will we get our clothes? How do we get from here to there? What happens if me and her boyfriend have a fight and we have to leave? If I leave the cops will be looking for me. I can't stay in the city too long. Unless you want me to go to jail. You would have to get used to me carrying a gun. I don't go anywhere unless I'm packin'. Who is paying for the apartment? How do we get around? Where do we get clothes from? I want to leave here so bad, but I'm not going anywhere unless I know what's up. When are you planning to leave anyway? We would have to figure that out real quick. What if she doesn't get to leave? Then what are we gonna do? Did you think about that? If I leave I don't plan on being caught anytime soon, so I have to know all of this stuff.

If we left we could be together as much as we want to though. Couldn't we? We could make love all of the time. As soon as you get me a good answer to these questions, I will tell you if we should go or not. You'll probably go even if I don't. If you did, I would find you and beat your ass!! I love you.

A. What was this person trying to do?

B. What tactic(s) was the groomer using?

C. How did this person want to make me feel?

D. What did this person want me to do?

E. How would I respond?

Letter 6

Hey sweetness. Miss me? Well I missed you! Today was my last day in that hell hole. I am so sorry that I made you angry for being there. I'll never ever go back. So were you being good when you didn't have me to cuddle or to make you feel good. Well I felt like I was losing you slowly but surely but I hope and pray that I don't. You'll never never lose me ever. There's nothing here that can steal my heart away from you, my lovely, my sweet. I did miss you a lot. I feel jealous when you sat at the table at lunch with that one guy. I felt that I had really messed up. I hope not cause I will always be with you and make you feel my presence wherever you go. You know how I feel. Hey baby. Listen, I'm gonna get straight to the point when are we gonna hook up at the movies or somethin' so we can do somethin' nasty. Cuz I've been wantin' to do somethin' to you for a long time! Ever since you first came here. So now you know. Write me back to let me know what you have to say. From me. I did call last night!

A. What was this person trying to do?

B. What tactic(s) was the groomer using?

C. How did this person want to make me feel?

D. What did this person want me to do?

E. How would I respond?

Letter 7

I LOVE YOU   I LOVE YOU

I told ***** to tell you I love you because I never have the right time to tell you, but I will today. Don't let ***** play with your head. Please don't leave me, I need you more than anything. We both love each other and don't want to lose each other, so we can't let nothing get in our way. You're my sweet thang forever. I want to find you right away and kiss you. Can I get a kiss after school. If I don't I think I will die. I'm glad we fell in love with each other, just thinking back to the first day I saw you. I wanted it to be us. And that's when I fell in love with you. Love at first sight. I knew we would get closer and closer. You mean a lot to me, don't give up on me for nothing. Remember I'm in love with you and I love you and we will stay TOGETHER FOREVER.

A. What was this person trying to do?

B. What tactic(s) was the groomer using?

C. How did this person want to make me feel?

D. What did this person want me to do?

E. How would I respond?

Letter 8

Hi sellout! Well anyways, about today. Meet me after school for a trip through the career center, to finish something we started. I'm sure you want a reason. Well, my reason is because I'm supposed to be gettin' the boot today for something I did over home visits! If you don't believe me, ask ***** or *****. I really wish we could be together.

All I'm askin' is "can we finish" so I can remember my last day with you? It's our last chance and besides no one would ever know. Because believe it or not, I began caring for you a lot!

Love = Me

P.S. Please let's do this the real proper way. So let's finish!

A. What was this person trying to do?

B. What tactic(s) was the groomer using?

C. How did this person want to make me feel?

D. What did this person want me to do?

E. How would I respond?

Letter 9

My dearest   ,

How are you doin'? Myself, I'm takin' it E.Z. I had a lovely time with you yesterday. You really lightened my day. I want you to know that I think you are a very attractive and sweet person. But, I am a lot older than you and where I come from they call it "robbin' the cradle." You know what I'm saying.

Even tho' age is just a number. I still like you and want to get to know you real good. If you know what I mean. I don't want any of these players up here trying to take advantage of you because you're young. I want to be there for you. If anybody gets you, it better be me. You're so special to me. Write back please.

A. What was this person trying to do?

B. What tactic(s) was the groomer using?

C. How did this person want to make me feel?

D. What did this person want me to do?

E. How would I respond?

Letter 10

Hi. How are you? Did you have fun with me last night. Yes or no. I had fun, but I wondered how you liked it? I will always love you baby. My mom found out about us. Now, I can't call boys and they can't call me. But, I will call you, OK? I will find a way. You are the only one who I love. I know I can trust you totally. And, I hope you had fun with me last night. You are nice and lovable and I think about you every day. I hope you will be there for me. I will give you anything you want and in a big way. If I can't have you I don't know what I'll do. I feel like killing myself right now. And I do hope I kill myself and sorry I said that.

A. What was this person trying to do?

B. What tactic(s) was the groomer using?

C. How did this person want to make me feel?

D. What did this person want me to do?

E. How would I respond?

Letter 11

Our relationship is going to last a long time. The feelings we have for each other are true. And will stay that way. If we start going out, we can't let others get in our way. Just remember I really do care about you in many different ways and I've fallen in love with you. You're all I want. We have to be honest with each other. And we can't tell anyone about us. You know how fast stuff spreads around here. Let's just keep it to ourselves and no one will ever need to know. I really care about you and I mean that. Have to get going.

A. What was this person trying to do?

B. What tactic(s) was the groomer using?

C. How did this person want to make me feel?

D. What did this person want me to do?

E. How would I respond?

Letter 12

This probably makes no sense to you, but I have some things I really need to tell you. I really wish I would have gotten your address. Can you send it to me?

Gosh, I don't know where to begin. I do like you (a lot). I did not know how to react or act around you. Don't get me wrong, it was not because you were black, but because you were a guy. See, I have never had a guy like me. Sure, as friends - most of my best friends are guys! It's just no one has ever done to me what you did. I was very overwhelmed and I did not know what to do. I thought you were so sweet and nice. I did not give you a fair chance. I wish I would have.

I know I am terrible at talking to guys, and I shouldn't really talk. It takes me awhile to get used to people and I took too long. I am so sorry. My mind wanted something with you, but something told me to hold on. Plus, a lot of people in my co-op told me that you would just use me and throw me away. I did not believe them, but I don't know. I really wish I could start over again.

Also, you always wore those sunglasses. I wanted to see your eyes. They were so understanding. I kind of was a little scared when you had the glasses on and your dark clothes and you told me to come there in the student center. You seemed like such a tough guy. I loved seeing your eyes. That's one of the things I loved about you.

I really could not figure you out because you were nice to me and everyone else just thinks of me as just a friend. Maybe I am making a lot out of nothing. But I just want you to know I liked you a lot.

A. What was this person trying to do?

B. What tactic(s) was the groomer using?

C. How did this person want to make me feel?

D. What did this person want me to do?

E. How would I respond?

Letter 13

So, he called you? What was his name? I know you at least know that. I've told her not to mess with me!!!! People get hurt when they mess with me. If I was getting another girl's number, that is between you, her and me. How in the hell did ***** get in it!!

I'm not mad at you, as long as you're not lying to me. If I find out you are lying, you and me are finished. So, if you're not telling me something, you better spill it now. I don't want to have to find out later from someone else. I can find out!!

You have to keep your friends out of our business. ***** is getting on my nerves. She is always in our business. Then whoever that was in your house that told you that shit the other day. I don't like shit like that. I don't let my friends get in my business like that. If this is our relationship they have to be out of it.

You are my lady, you will be until you give me a reason to feel differently. I'm not mad at you. You haven't gave me a reason to be. Unless I find out you're lying to me. If I find out you are, be ready, because I'm going off. That's why I said if you left something out, tell me now.

I still love you. I'm not mad at you. I'm gonna go off on *****, though. She is gonna stay out of my business. If not she'll get her ass hurt. I can't stand people fucking around with me. I gotta go. Love ya.

A. What was this person trying to do?

B. What tactic(s) was the groomer using?

C. How did this person want to make me feel?

D. What did this person want me to do?

E. How would I respond?

Letter 14

I'm telling you now and one time only, I want his shit out of your locker. What kind of fool do I look like? I'm going out with you, but your ex-boyfriend is still in your locker. No!! That is not going to happen. I want his stuff out. Today! What did you say to ***** today? She is messing with me. She's getting on my nerves. Your friend better go somewhere. If she messes with me I'll fuck her up. You better get his stuff out of your locker!! If you're my girl his shit has to go. If you want him it can stay. Your choice. Peace.

A. What was this person trying to do?

B. What tactic(s) was the groomer using?

C. How did this person want to make me feel?

D. What did this person want me to do?

E. How would I respond?

Letter 15

Hey BABY what's down. Shit, it's 11:45 and I can't sleep at all. Maybe it's because I feel so bad about what I did to you. But maybe we can start all over. We shouldn't have gotten caught. We won't be able to see each other as much. But then if it does we can still be secret lovers. And no one would have to know about it and it would just be our little secret. You know how much I care about you and hope you feel the same way. I love you more than words can say. But it's hard for me to give you my feelings here.

Today was the most depressing day I had in my life. When I wanted to listen to the radio all I would hear is songs that made it worse for me to start feeling normal again. But hey, I probably will have a lot more of these kinds of situations. What I'm going to say is going to be real hard for me to say. But I made many other girls hurt, and cry because I would go out on them or do stupid things. But I really didn't give a shit. All I would do is just laugh when I heard they cried over me. But with you I couldn't laugh or just didn't forget about it. This shows that I really hurt someone who I love and care about. And you've been on my mind all day. And I am very sorry for leading you on like the way I did. And just doing what I did.

But you know I'll take the offer of being together for ever. No matter what happens to us I just want you to know if you need anybody to love or just talk to when you are down. I will always be available. But it is going to be up to you if you want to marry me. Please write back, but be careful that no one knows about us.

A. What was this person trying to do?

B. What tactic(s) was the groomer using?

C. How did this person want to make me feel?

D. What did this person want me to do?

E. How would I respond?

Letter 16

Hi, what's up? Me, not too much, just that I miss you. I know you might think I'm an asshole for all the stuff I did to you and I'm sorry. Well, I guess you know by now, I'm not coming back because of all the junk I did. But, I'll be going home in no time at all and I would like for us to get back together. If you don't mind having a boyfriend off campus. Because before I got kicked out, I wanted to get back with you before I left, but I didn't know I'd be leaving. I still love you and ain't anything going to change it.

When I was going with *****, I could not take my mind off you. I know I messed up by letting you go and I might not get you back. But I'm asking you to give me one more chance. We could have a better relationship now that I'll be home. I could meet you on your outings.

I'm really sorry for the stuff I did to you. Sorry! And I plan on making it up to you. So what do you think? I'll treat you right and I'm not going to do anything behind your back. You are what I live for. So without you my soul is black and my heart is empty.

It might sound like I'm trying to get over on you but I'm not. I mean everything I say. It comes from the heart. I cry just about every night hoping I could be with you. You're the best girl I ever had and I lost you. But I'm asking for one more chance to be with you and treat you like a Queen should be treated. And a Queen is what you is. A Queen that I need in my life to keep me out of trouble and if you look back you can see I did not really start getting in trouble until I let you go. Please come back to me, I need you.

A. What was this person trying to do?

B. What tactic(s) was the groomer using?

C. How did this person want to make me feel?

D. What did this person want me to do?

E. How would I respond?

Letter 17

I just thought I'd tell you that you'll never find another person like me who loves with all of their heart. I guess I see now that you haven't noticed. It hurts so much inside. I want it to go away. Talk to me openly and honestly so I'll understand the most important question in my life, am I still an important person in your life? Please tell me because sometimes I don't know whether to stay or to go. You need to choose who you want to be with the most and be loyal to them. If the other people aren't happy, then I guess they never did like you. I'm lost. I don't know what to do. Sometimes I feel you don't understand the real me. I try to let you find me, but it seems you never want to. Well, gotta cruise. Keep in touch. Love lasts forever.

A. What was this person trying to do?

B. What tactic(s) was the groomer using?

C. How did this person want to make me feel?

D. What did this person want me to do?

E. How would I respond?

Letter 18

You mean a lot to me. You are the only boy I want to be with. When you said we should start talking to other people, I thought I was going to die. I don't want you to go out with someone else. I don't know what I would do. It's all up to you. ***** and I had a long talk after school, and I told him how I feel about you and nothing was going to stop me from talking to you. The way you were acting last week, I thought you were just playing with my mind. If you knew how much I cared about you, you might change your mind. I can't stop thinking about what you said about being friends. I don't want you as a friend, I see you as a special friend. I would do anything to be with you and I mean that. Please write back. I need to hear an answer.

A. What was this person trying to do?

B. What tactic(s) was the groomer using?

C. How did this person want to make me feel?

D. What did this person want me to do?

E. How would I respond?

Letter 19

We can't let anyone break us apart. If we get into an argument or disagreement we will work it out. People here can't be trusted. Only trust me. I couldn't wait to ask you out so I did it on the phone. I didn't get to say all I wanted but I said the most important thing. But I still will ask you in your face and do it the right way. You mean a lot to me and we can't let anyone break us apart. I don't want to lose you for anything. I think I would kill myself if I lost you. You mean everything to me. Don't let people break us apart for anything.

A. What was this person trying to do?

B. What tactic(s) was the groomer using?

C. How did this person want to make me feel?

D. What did this person want me to do?

E. How would I respond?

Letter 20

I was so happy to hear your voice on the phone last night. When I get home, if I see you I will give you something I've been wanting to give you for the longest time. Even though you said I could do something with a girl for one day, I won't because I only want you. I only want one girl and that's you.

What would you do if I kissed you? Would you hit me or kiss me back? I was just wondering because I might just do it one day. You have to hurry up and get on weekly so we can go out to the movies sometimes. I hope I will be able to see you. We really do want to be with each other. I did something bad after I got off the phone, but it wasn't with a girl. I would never do anything to hurt you or do anything behind your back. You mean too much to me to let you go. I won't let anyone get in our relationship. It's hard for me to tell someone I love them. But I could tell you because I care about you, you care about me, and I could finally be open to someone I love a lot I mean every word I say to you from the bottom of my heart. I could go on forever telling you how much I want to be with you, but I won't because you already know how I feel about you.

A. What was this person trying to do?

B. What tactic(s) was the groomer using?

C. How did this person want to make me feel?

D. What did this person want me to do?

E. How would I respond?

Letter 21

I know a lot of guys like me but I don't like them. I do want to keep this low for awhile so I don't build a bad rep. You know what I'm sayin'. You seem like a nice person to me. I hope that one day you and I will be closer together. You look good and you know it. I understand that you want a fine babe like me, so don't get all choked up. You treat me right and you'll see what that brings you. Don't you dare let anyone read this letter.

P.S. Remember keep this LOW!

A. What was this person trying to do?

B. What tactic(s) was the groomer using?

C. How did this person want to make me feel?

D. What did this person want me to do?

E. How would I respond?

Letter 22

You are such a sweetheart!

Wuz up? Well, with me there's not much going on if I must say. Don't you trust me in many ways? Do you think that if you and I ever did something together that I would tell someone else?

I wouldn't dare tell anyone anything you tell me. I believe in you too much to let you down. It's been about 2 1/2 months since I got a letter from you. And here is your answers to the questions okay, baby doll,

1. Do I still like you, of course I do. I like you more than just a friend.

2. ***** and I are just friends okay and nothing else.

3. Well, I think that you are a wonderful person and I do admire you for your sweetness. I think of you as an angel to me because I adore the things you do and the way you do them. I know that you are absolutely lovely and I really mean it when I say that you are worth the time.

4. If I had the chance of going out with you again, I would take the chance because you were and still is the best girl out of all my girls that I've had and I'm really serious about that also. Although we aren't going out, you always make me feel good and wanted.

You are just simply the sweetest. I hope that you're being treated fairly by *****. I wish that we had never broken up. Do you still like me like I do? I want our friendship to carry on like it's been going so far. By the way, do you still wanna go on the outing together? I just wouldn't want to miss that. I'll always be good to you because I care for you also sweetheart. Always stay the way you are just for me and keep young and beautiful okay baby cakes. You are on my mind. I'll call you baby cakes from now on if you don't mind! I don't know what I want for my birthday but anything will do okay baby cakes. 2 of us 2 gether and 4 ever. To my "crystal." Luv You. From your "diamond."

A. What was this person trying to do?

B. What tactic(s) was the groomer using?

C. How did this person want to make me feel?

D. What did this person want me to do?

E. How would I respond?

Letter 23

How are you doing. I'm fine. Could be better. It feels good to talk to you on the phone. Maybe it will be better when we talk face to face. It's not that I'm using *****, it's just that I can talk to my friends if I want to. I like her, yes. She's leaving and its going to be hard for her to leave because she says she likes me a lot. But I can't tell if she does or not. I've talked to you for two days. I think you're a very nice person and you and me will become good friends or more. I can't tell how things are going to be. I can tell you one thing, I'm not a player. It's that a lot of these girls are like you. They like what they see and I can't help that, right? There's guys that think you're hot. I do. I just don't want other guys trying to start a relationship with you just to use you. I won't. If someone gets to start a relationship with you, I won't fight them or anything. I just want them to treat you well. You deserve that. I know I would treat you fine. See you later, I have to get some sleep. Write back.

A. What was this person trying to do?

B. What tactic(s) was the groomer using?

C. How did this person want to make me feel?

D. What did this person want me to do?

E. How would I respond?

Letter 24

Smile, laugh and think about it!! Stopping by to say a word or two. Hi! How are ya sweet thing? I'm doing okay I guess. Why don't you understand me at times? I wanted to talk to you after school but you left because of *****. We are not talking, in fact she's going out with this ***** guy and I was only signing her book. By the way I'm sorry if I did something that might have gotten you upset. I was unable to use the phone and I also couldn't go to the field house because of this ***** girl. Anyways, you may feel as if I only want one thing from you but that's totally untrue.

If you feel as if I'm leading you on, maybe I shouldn't call or bother you then because I don't want to be guilty of anything. It's all up to you to decide what you wanna do. Maybe I'm getting in your way or something? Am I or am I not? I do like you a lot even though we're not going out. If I didn't would I waste my 5 minutes of phone call on you? Would I call you when there's a lot more girls that I could be calling or would I even talk to you?

I'm not too good for you at all because there's no such thing. *****, please believe me I do care and like you and I wouldn't be wasting my time if I didn't. I know what you mean and I do understand too but I sometimes wonder where should I start. I don't want you to get in a position where you'll feel all confused because I want you to be happy. Think about it okay!! Gots to go for now and I'll see ya later. Love you lots!

A. What was this person trying to do?

B. What tactic(s) was the groomer using?

C. How did this person want to make me feel?

D. What did this person want me to do?

E. How would I respond?

Letter 25

What you said earlier at the picnic keeps repeating itself over and over in my mind. About love, kids and us. Please believe me. It's not you at all. It's me. Number one. My self esteem ain't the best, it's very low. Two, I'm not really positive when a guy loves me for me or for some other reason. Three, I'm scared. Because every other male liked me for sex, popularity, looks or something else.

I do love you, *****. I love every moment we spend together even if it is when I get annoyed with you. I still love you. I just hate not being able to touch you. That's why your kiss surprised me so much and every time you touch me I feel warm inside and when I'm with you I feel like it is for real. You really love me for me and there was no other guys before who hurt me, there's only you. Then when you leave I feel insecure again and I feel like crying because I'm scared you'll leave me for someone else. And hurt me again.

I do want to have a child. A boy. And it's painful to know that there's a 99% chance I can't because of miscarriages and other reasons. You tripped me out when you said lets leave and go do that. I swear you were kidding. When I think someone's serious I'll usually go do it. But no one here is usually serious. I wanted to believe you were serious. I would of gone in a heartbeat if I thought you were.

That's the first time you ever told me how much you loved me so I could hear it. Not write it but told me. And I felt so good inside. Like when you touch me. Hopefully, soon time will come for us to be together for a long, long time. Maybe forever. I want you to remember that okay? I love you.

A. What was this person trying to do?

B. What tactic(s) was the groomer using?

C. How did this person want to make me feel?

D. What did this person want me to do?

E. How would I respond?

Letter 26

What's up my love? I have been thinking about you night and day. I've been thinking about how much I love you which is a lot Some other things I've been thinking about is when I first saw you and when I held you in my arms in back of the school. I miss you so much. I can't wait to see you again. There's a lot of things I love about you. You're smart, you have a sweet personality and you are very pretty.

You are very special to me. Just thinking about you makes me happy. I really want to be there for you. You are too sweet to be taken advantage of and treated bad. And I don't want that to happen. I do like to do it, but, we are going to take it nice slow. You know what I'm saying. Some time I will show you how much I love you, but not right now. Gotta go.

A. What was this person trying to do?

B. What tactic(s) was the groomer using?

C. How did this person want to make me feel?

D. What did this person want me to do?

E. How would I respond?

Letter 27

I'm just thinking about you and how pretty you are. I really like you a lot. I feel like asking you out but that would have been going too fast. I don't want to do anything to get you in trouble. Do you want to start talking? If we start talking, we can't be talking for 8 months and that's all if you know what I mean. You're all I think about and I'm not saying that just to make you like me more. I'm writing this to let you know how I feel about you, and I mean every word I say to you. I was telling ***** about how I feel about you and he said he was going to start talking to you because he likes you too. But, I'm not going to let him get in my way of talking to you. He's not for you. He may do something to hurt you and I won't. He plays on all of the girls he has ever gone out with. Stay away from him. You are very pretty and I mean that. If we were going out, I would want you to know I would never do anything to hurt you.

A. What was this person trying to do?

B. What tactic(s) was the groomer using?

C. How did this person want to make me feel?

D. What did this person want me to do?

E. How would I respond?

Letter 28

Hey sweetness, how are ya? Me, okay I guess. I had a great day yesterday with you. That's the way I want you to treat me. Like a good friend. So, we're still going out, aren't we? I hope so. I was so happy that you asked me out. I've wanted you to do that for the longest time. Oh! Yesterday, did ***** find out what we did after school? I thought I was busted because of them. It was really strange when you said, "If I have sex with you, I'll have to be with you forever." Why did you say that? Do you want to do that so we can be together forever? That would be so great, but your parents suck. They won't give us another chance. I hope this time our relationship lasts, even if they don't like it. Sorry for leaving yesterday after school. I wish I could have stayed with you forever, but you know those stupid rules. This is so great. We're together still after all the problems in the past. Now we have to look at the present and deal with it in a positive way so we can be together. There's one thing I got to ask of you - please, whatever you do, don't hurt me. I love you too much to be hurt by you. That means if you see me in the hall, don't just walk by me. Another thing, will you please not write ***** and ***** anymore? If they ask you why you don't write them, say, "I don't have time." I'm not saying you can't talk to them. You can, that's fine, but if you see me, I'd appreciate it if you'd talk to me. Well, later up! Love always.

A. What was this person trying to do?

B. What tactic(s) was the groomer using?

C. How did this person want to make me feel?

D. What did this person want me to do?

E. How would I respond?

Letter 29

Hi honey. How are you. When I said I would give you something special, I take that back. I don't want you to think anything about that. I want you to do good cause hopefully you'd feel good and that would make me feel good. Speaking of good asses, you got a nice one yourself. I like you for what you are not what you can give. It's just that sometimes when I'm around you I feel like doing this and that. I want to get closer and stuff and don't do all this negative stuff. Then nature can take its time. Let's get closer but don't go too far. I want you badly. But I will wait if I have to. I have other stuff to say but I don't want to write it down.

A. What was this person trying to do?

B. What tactic(s) was the groomer using?

C. How did this person want to make me feel?

D. What did this person want me to do?

E. How would I respond?

Letter 30

What's Up?

How are you doin' sweetheart? Myself, thinking about you mostly. I wish I could be with you so much. I called you back last night and your mom answered the phone and she told me that I couldn't call you anymore because I was too old to talk to you. I know you don't like that any more than I do but I promise you we will work around that. Because I like you too much and no matter what anybody says, I will always be there for you. Nobody can keep us apart. I want you to be my girl. I want to ask you face to face so you can see for yourself how serious I am. I love you and I want you to be happy. You deserve a lot of tender lovin' care, and I want to be the one to give it to you. That's from the bottom of my heart.

A. What was this person trying to do?

B. What tactic(s) was the groomer using?

C. How did this person want to make me feel?

D. What did this person want me to do?

E. How would I respond?

Letter 31

I know you are coming back from the lake tomorrow. So I will call you and see how you are doing and to talk about our relationship. We do make a good couple if you ask me. I just got me a Michael Jordan jump suit. I was going to try and get you one, but I don't have any money right now. But I get paid 60 dollars Friday if it all works out. My parents will be watching how I spend it so I'll have to think of something. I have fallen in love with you and I mean that. I can't wait to see you because I have something for you and I have to do something. It's a surprise. And I'm not going to tell, I will just wait for the right time. I hope you will like it, I know you will. I've been in the house all day watching TV and being bored. Have you told ***** about us? I know if you tell her or anybody else they would be happy for you. Because a lot of people said we make a good couple and that's the truth. I won't let you get away from me anymore cause I love you and yes I do love you. I can't wait till you see your surprise!

A. What was this person trying to do?

B. What tactic(s) was the groomer using?

C. How did this person want to make me feel?

D. What did this person want me to do?

E. How would I respond?

Letter 32

Did you get the tape I made for you. I mixed it myself. All of the songs on there remind me of you. I especially like the one that says I can't wait 2 get 2 school each day, and wait for you to pass my way, and the bells start to ring, an angel starts 2 say, Hey that's the girl for you, so what are you gonna do, hey little girl I love you. All I do is think of you day and night that's all I do. I can't get you off my mind. Think about you all the time, all the time girl. I've begun 2 take the long way home just so I can be alone 2 think of how 2 say my heart is here to stay.

If I could do it I'd buy you everything you wanted. Remember that sweater at the mall. That would look so good on you baby. Someday I'll buy it or steal it if I have to. You mean the world to me and I want to show you how much. Well it's late and I'd better get to bed.

A. What was this person trying to do?

B. What tactic(s) was the groomer using?

C. How did this person want to make me feel?

D. What did this person want me to do?

E. How would I respond?

Letter 33

I'm just sitting in bed thinking about our relationship. I feel that we are going to get closer and closer fast. I wish I could give you something before I leave if you know what I mean. I will miss you and I will be thinking about you every second of the day. I care about you in many different ways, and I mean that from the bottom of my heart. I wish I could see you right now, and tell you how much I want and need you. I don't want to lose you for anything. We can't be lettin' other people try to keep us from getting closer. We are made for each other. The song that makes me think about our relationship is One More Try. It's all about us that's why I like it. I won't do anything to hurt you and I won't mess with any girls because I want to be with one person. And that's you. Trust me. You don't do anything bad, if you know what I mean. I will miss you a lot. I love you in many ways.

A. What was this person trying to do?

B. What tactic(s) was the groomer using?

C. How did this person want to make me feel?

D. What did this person want me to do?

E. How would I respond?

Letter 34

I'm just chillin out with the home boyz, and staying out of trouble, as usual. If only I could see you now and show you how much I miss you. I keep calling everyday, but someone is always on the phone. I've been going to the mall and I'm going to a party Friday. And, I won't do anything wrong (such as girls). I wish I had a picture of you so I could look at you and hold it close to my heart. I keep thinking about what I said to you on the phone, about how I wasn't going to mess with any girls. Well, I haven't. So that means you have to do the same thing. I'm not saying you're not, but, you know what I'm saying. I'm not letting you get away from me anymore. I'm in love with you. And I'll be good to you. Remember that.

A. What was this person trying to do?

B. What tactic(s) was the groomer using?

C. How did this person want to make me feel?

D. What did this person want me to do?

E. How would I respond?

Letter 35

I'm doing nothing but watching TV and doing homework. Just thinking about you, I start smiling because you mean a lot to me. Now that I have fallen in love with you. I can't wait to see you because I'm going to ask you out right then and there. We have to be honest with each other all the time. Don't ever run away because you will just get in a lot of trouble. But if you want to sneak out and see me, that's OK, but don't get caught. I wish I could see you right now. The way I see it, you want to be with me, and I want to be with you. That says we are made for each other. You are more important than anything in my life. So remember that. You're mine from here on. If you want to sneak out just tell me when so I can be outside. We might get caught if we go in the house. Love.

A. What was this person trying to do?

B. What tactic(s) was the groomer using?

C. How did this person want to make me feel?

D. What did this person want me to do?

E. How would I respond?

Letter 36

You mean a lot to me in so many ways. I hope you like the pictures. I'm love sick not seeing you. When I saw you in church, I wanted to give you a big hug and kiss. That new girl kept looking at me like she likes me. But don't worry. If only you were here right now, I'd give you something you'd never forget. Are you thinking about me right now, because I just can't stop thinking about you and how pretty you are. I'm going to kick *****'s ass if he doesn't quit hitting on you. Do you like him? I don't want him to come between us. I think about you all the time.

A. What was this person trying to do?

B. What tactic(s) was the groomer using?

C. How did this person want to make me feel?

D. What did this person want me to do?

E. How would I respond?

Letter 37

I'm so happy because I will be able to see you tomorrow. Did you miss me, because I missed you. I know we've only known each other for five days, but I want to treat you right. You're the first girl I've ever fallen in love with so fast. We need to get together to talk about our relationship. See if I can come over one day. I know you'll be able to come over here but your ***** are different. You should start going to the Field House more so we can see each other more. I made a song about you and me. It's good, I'll let you hear it one day. As soon as I see you, I'm going to ask you out because I can't wait anymore. When are you going to give me a picture of you? I don't care if you just woke up or look dead, just give me one. I love you so much, and I know you will love me if you just give me a chance. Closer, closer, closer, closer.

A. What was this person trying to do?

B. What tactic(s) was the groomer using?

C. How did this person want to make me feel?

D. What did this person want me to do?

E. How would I respond?

Letter 38

I know that we've only been talking for two days, but I want to tell you how fine I think you are. You make me feel like no one else ever has in my life. Can you meet me behind the Field House tonight. I just want to talk to you in private with no one else around so I can tell you how I really feel. I won't do anything else, I promise. You will know that I can be trusted when you get to know me better. I would never hurt you or anything like that. Let me know if you can meet me.

A. What was this person trying to do?

B. What tactic(s) was the groomer using?

C. How did this person want to make me feel?

D. What did this person want me to do?

E. How would I respond?

Letter 39

What's up? Not much this way. Just chillin' out at work writing you this note. So you and ***** gonna start goin' out? I was just wondering because if you weren't I'd like to get with you. I've always had this thing about fine girls. You and me would be a great couple. Well, anyway, what has ***** been saying about me? She's alright but I don't think I would go out with her. She's not fine enough for me. Anyway, you haven't told me anything about you. The only thing I know is that you are from ********. Well, think about you and me getting together. Let's just keep you and me a secret, OK?

A. What was this person trying to do?

B. What tactic(s) was the groomer using?

C. How did this person want to make me feel?

D. What did this person want me to do?

E. How would I respond?

Letter 40

I tried to call you so many times yesterday. Every time I call you someone is always on it. I'll give you some pictures of me so you can look at them before you go to bed. Don't play me like a sucker again, that pisses me off. Plus I won't let you because I want you more than anyone does.

A. What was this person trying to do?

B. What tactic(s) was the groomer using?

C. How did this person want to make me feel?

D. What did this person want me to do?

E. How would I respond?

Letter 41

I went over to my friends house this morning to see if he was going to buy the speakers still. I lowered the price to 25 dollars. It's hard for me to stay out of trouble. We bought half a stick of dynamite yesterday, from some drunk man. How much do you have left on daily, so we can go out. It's 12:15 a.m. right now and we just got through egging cars and houses. I didn't get caught so don't worry about it. I can't sleep because it's too hot and I'm thinking about you. Do you think I could come over to your house one day or you could come over to mine? I want to be with you for a long time. Do you want to be with me for a long time? Maybe you could help me stay out of trouble. You would be so good for me. Just remember I want you and no one else.

A. What was this person trying to do?

B. What tactic(s) was the groomer using?

C. How did this person want to make me feel?

D. What did this person want me to do?

E. How would I respond?

Letter 42

What's up. I'm just sitting on the bed thinking about what I should do to you the next time I see you. I miss you so much and I feel like I'm going to die if I don't see you. Tell me that we have gotten real close. I feel like I've known you forever. I collect the "Love Is" cartoons and I have certain ones for you. I know you would like them. I was just thinking about what you would do if I tried to kiss you. What would you do if I tried something else. Not saying I will, just wondering. Think about it.

A. What was this person trying to do?

B. What tactic(s) was the groomer using?

C. How did this person want to make me feel?

D. What did this person want me to do?

E. How would I respond?

Letter 43

A lot of people are happy that we're talking and I am very happy. I'm sorry that I haven't been spending a lot of time with you, because of *****. I'll tell her somehow that I don't want to talk to her anymore. It will be hard because she likes me a lot, but I have to tell her, because I want to talk to one person and that's you. I just don't want to hurt anyone that's all. That's the type of guy I am. You're all I think about. I think about you every second of the day. I am real sorry. When you were mad at me, I didn't know what to do because you wouldn't talk to me. And then I saw you talking with *****, and I thought you were talking. I don't want to lose you to anybody else. So are we still talking or can I ask you out? We are a fine couple together, no doubt about it. A lot of people have told me that. You are sweet and so sexy too.

A. What was this person trying to do?

B. What tactic(s) was the groomer using?

C. How did this person want to make me feel?

D. What did this person want me to do?

E. How would I respond?

Letter 44

I'm just sitting in bed thinking about all the stuff we talked about over the phone. I know we haven't known each other that long, but since we have talked for 2 days, it seems like I know you like the back of my hand. I really like you a lot and I mean that from the bottom of my heart. I'm not like *****, trying to just get some, if you know what I mean. I wanted to talk to you when you first got here, but I didn't know how. I wish we were talking right now. But you're still with *****. Are you going to tell him that you don't want to talk anymore? If you do, we can't start seeing each other right away, because he'll know something is up. Would you start talking with me if I asked you? You're all I think about now. I'm always thinking about things we could do, if you know what I mean.

P.S. Don't show this to anyone, OK.

A. What was this person trying to do?

B. What tactic(s) was the groomer using?

C. How did this person want to make me feel?

D. What did this person want me to do?

E. How would I respond?

Letter 45

Hey, hi. Well, I'm sorry I didn't write until now, but I was real busy with senior homework. You understand, don't ya? Well, I can't wait till we're able to spend some real time together. You know what I'm sayin' too! But anyways, you're gonna have a baby by me once I leave from here, so be prepared! I can't wait to rescue another kiss from you! *****, I believe we could possibly turn out to be somethin' special. You know what I'm sayin'. Well honey, I must go now, ok!

I'll call you before I bust a move to the game!

Love = Me

A. What was this person trying to do?

B. What tactic(s) was the groomer using?

C. How did this person want to make me feel?

D. What did this person want me to do?

E. How would I respond?

Letter 46

What's up? I'm just sitting in the basement thinking about you, and how long we've been talking. I'm glad we are, because I like you a lot. ***** wants me to ask you out, but I told her that that would be rushing it too fast. I want to, but as I said it would be rushing it. ***** really wants to go out with me, but I don't know how to say NO, but I will somehow. That's why you see me with her, because of the problems we had together. She wants to talk about them. That's all, we're just talking. If I asked you out would you say "Yes," "No," or "Why." You can't be getting into trouble and losing your privileges because I need to talk to you. I think if we went out together we would last a long time if we don't let other people or problems break us apart.

Sometimes I can't sleep at night because I think about you and other relationships I've had and what I would do to you. But mostly I think about what we could do together. We would be fine together. When you told me about what happened to you back home, I couldn't stop thinking about why someone would want to beat you. I hate hearing things like that, I just want you to know I would never do anything to hurt you.

A. What was this person trying to do?

B. What tactic(s) was the groomer using?

C. How did this person want to make me feel?

D. What did this person want me to do?

E. How would I respond?

Letter 47

What's down? Nothing here, but the earth that has a sweet and special young lady on it named *****! Well, I'm just laying here listening to Boys to Men, "Please Don't Go Away From Me" and thinking about the other night we expressed some of our feelings for each other in a physical way! That kept me warm and made me feel relaxed. And I felt so good with you lying in my arms, as I played with your hair and ran my hands across your ever so soft body! But, the main part I keep in my mind is when I was about to go and you asked for a hug good-bye. And I was kneeling on the bed, and as I pulled you closer to me, the light from the windows behind me was shining on your beautiful eyes that seemed to be sparkling with happiness as I pulled you even closer and then kissed your soft lips! It was from that point on since I feel that you do like me!!

I'm glad that you let me know your feelings for me in your letters that you write to me. Because some girls like you, and they never tell you nothing. So, then you don't know if they really care for you or not. So, keep letting me know how you feel about me, okay?

Everything has just been going so well between us. I hope it will last a long time. but, I also know we will have our bad times. But, if we care for each other enough, we will get over all of the bad things. So, if you ever feel mad at me, or you are upset about something, just let me know what's up! Because I would really want to know what I did wrong so I can correct my mistake!

Well, I just want you to know that I do care for you, and I know you are a really nice person. So, now I am about to go, so write back as soon as possible and make it good!

P.S. I am gonna call you Twinkles.

A. What was this person trying to do?

B. What tactic(s) was the groomer using?

C. How did this person want to make me feel?

D. What did this person want me to do?

E. How would I respond?

Letter 48

Hey Sweet thang. What's down. Not much here. Just got done with my homework. You know I felt like grabbing you and just start making out right there in that little room. But I didn't cause there were too many people around. So what I'm saying is that we need to be alone. Meet me after school today and we'll go somewhere and then I can get my kiss.

I think you should start doing better. And then you can come with me to the movies. Or not with me but meet me at the movie theater. You know what I mean.

Well, I don't know what else to write cause I'm having a bad day. But I love you. And if you ever need a shoulder to lean on or just a hug and someone to talk to, I'll be there when you need me. And yes, I know the situation is sneaky but who cares. I'll stay with you anyway, no matter what. You can also hold me whenever you want, any time. And when I look at you I say to myself, don't let this one get away. But I love you very much.

A friend and secret love,

Don't let no one see this letter, it's our secret.

A. What was this person trying to do?

B. What tactic(s) was the groomer using?

C. How did this person want to make me feel?

D. What did this person want me to do?

E. How would I respond?

Letter 49

Hey good lookin'! What's up? I was really excited talking to you on the phone tonight. I haven't talked to you in a long time. I couldn't believe we kissed right where we did today. We could have gotten busted big time. I think we better be more careful in the future, like when there's no one around, or you're walking me to the field house 5th period, or after school down by the food services door. I just don't want to get busted because if I do, I don't know what my teachers will say to me.

How come you wouldn't take your picture with me at Homecoming? I really want some more pictures of you, as many as ***** has of you. I also would really like a picture of you and me together. I think your house should have a party and you said your parents aren't that strict, so maybe we could get busy. I don't know why I've been acting so strange lately, but I have been wanting sex put it that way. Well what do you think about that. Well I better break so I can go to sleep and dream about you. I wish I could dream about you and remember it, but I can't. How do I know you care and love me if you never tell me you do?

A. What was this person trying to do?

B. What tactic(s) was the groomer using?

C. How did this person want to make me feel?

D. What did this person want me to do?

E. How would I respond?

Letter 50

For these gorgeous eyes of yours only!

What's kickin' hon? Just peeking to say a word or two. I'm badly in need of enjoying the most happiest moments with you alone. The fun and pleasure begins with what you have and therefore it's quite out of reach. There's nothing I'd like to do more than kissing your gentle lips and slightly pulling your tongue with compassion.

Most likely I'd want to touch you all over and see if you're really ticklish. I want to put my legs between your thighs and do the wild thing.

Loneliness won't leave me alone and I feel like being with you every second of the day having fun and also playing with your belly button your face is so smooth which wants to make me put my arms around you and run my fingers through your hair. I'll give you more than you want and can take. If only this would come true.

I don't want to go on without your love and beauty. I'll be waiting for your call anytime. There's a job that has to be done and I really want to work on your body.

I do love and want you. The next time I ever kiss you, there will be a difference in it. So keep cute just for me okay. Love ya all the time. I can't wait too long. To my sweetness. You're my lover girl!

A. What was this person trying to do?

B. What tactic(s) was the groomer using?

C. How did this person want to make me feel?

D. What did this person want me to do?

E. How would I respond?

Letter 51

You know you said you will do anything for me. Let me see what you can do. Don't show a single soul this letter especially not *****. Cause I don't want her giving you a bunch of shit, which she will. Please don't show anyone, please. And at AA I will get the kiss I never had the chance to get. You will have your socks knocked off by me. And don't go out with *****. He's going to hurt you more and I don't want to see you get hurt. I think all he thinks about sex. You need a man of sensitivity and that's me. Don't think I couldn't get loose around you, because I could. I could make you feel real good if I got the chance. See you later, gotta go.

A. What was this person trying to do?

B. What tactic(s) was the groomer using?

C. How did this person want to make me feel?

D. What did this person want me to do?

E. How would I respond?

Letter 52

If you get in trouble doing anything wrong and I hear about it, you will deal with me. I don't want to do anything with any other girl except you. I'm the only one who is right for you. So don't play on me, OK. You wouldn't want to see me mad. Our relationship is working out real fine right now and we're getting closer and closer. Don't mess it up. We have real feelings for one another. Just do what I say and everything will be alright.

A. What was this person trying to do?

B. What tactic(s) was the groomer using?

C. How did this person want to make me feel?

D. What did this person want me to do?

E. How would I respond?

Letter 53

I didn't say you did anything. But just tell me or not if you did anything with *****. If you want him, just go out with him. I'll get over it. It's not like you would really care anyway. You can't say that I've did anything to ***** cause I didn't. You can believe any damned person you want to. I didn't do shit to her. ***** even came up to me and said some things about you and him, and what you did.

Don't do this to me, even when I hear this stuff, it hurts my feelings. No, that's not all I want either and who ever you been hearing this from is lying or something. I guess it's no big deal. I just don't think I'm really your type or good enough for you. I'm screwing too many things up. I'm not worth it. So let me know if you want to stop our relationship, I'll try to understand. I probably deserve it anyway. The way I treat you, I'm not doing it the way I'm supposed to. I guess I was wrong. I'm sorry for treating you the way I did.

A. What was this person trying to do?

B. What tactic(s) was the groomer using?

C. How did this person want to make me feel?

D. What did this person want me to do?

E. How would I respond?

Letter 54

What's going on? Thanks for coming to my football game. I didn't know you were gonna come. I would have pulled up my shirt but then I thought I would look dumb pulling up my shirt. I would have given you some pictures of me but I can't find them anywhere. I have some coming on the way. Another thing, I sacrifice myself staying up all late and things, just to write you something. What do you do in return? I have some ideas. I'll tell you if you want to know. Another thing, I'm sorry for overreacting. I shouldn't have done that. I was really mad. And when I get mad I don't know what I'll do. Thanks for putting up with it. Why are you hitting on ***** for? I mean, you can talk to whoever you want but doing something else is another thing. Don't play around on me. I don't like it. I was wondering if you get mad if I write to ***** or not. She asked me to write her. I hope you're doing OK. Well, I'll write more later.

A. What was this person trying to do?

B. What tactic(s) was the groomer using?

C. How did this person want to make me feel?

D. What did this person want me to do?

E. How would I respond?

Letter 55

So what's up Sweet Cakes. Not much here, just chillin' in English reading this boring story. So what's going on with us. Don't say you don't know, because I notice a lot of guys like you. I don't want to be sharing a girl. I want you to know that I do like you and I wouldn't mind getting to know you a lot better. There's probably a lot that goes around about me that you hear, but I hope you don't believe it. If there is anything that you do believe or are curious about, then feel free to ask me and I swear I will tell you the honest truth. You seem like a very nice person who would be a good friend also. (You look great too!!) If you can call me, call. So when you get a chance to tell me if we could get together let me know. Don't believe everything you hear about me unless you ask me if it's true. We'd be a good couple.

A. What was this person trying to do?

B. What tactic(s) was the groomer using?

C. How did this person want to make me feel?

D. What did this person want me to do?

E. How would I respond?

Letter 56

How are you doin'? Myself, I'm not so doing too good, especially after I heard a few things about you from *****. Tomorrow ***** is supposed to be telling me some things about you. What kind of girl are you anyway. Your past isn't very good. If there is something you need to tell me, please do. I know that we haven't gone out yet, but I don't want to lose you. I have already decided that I want you and nobody else. And I hope you feel the same way. I don't want to hear a bunch of stuff about you from someone else. It makes me so mad, I don't know what I will do. I want to kick somebody's ass when I hear things about you. You need to be honest with me and let me know the truth. If you can, please try and call me tomorrow. I love you a lot, keep that in mind.

A. What was this person trying to do?

B. What tactic(s) was the groomer using?

C. How did this person want to make me feel?

D. What did this person want me to do?

E. How would I respond?